The Cats of

A MOSTLY PEACEABLE KINGDOM

Photographs by Dave and Jennifer McMichael

Additional photographs by Mimi Vang Olsen

SIMON & SCHUSTER
New York   London   Toronto   Sydney   Tokyo   Singapore

ROGER A. CARAS

Thistle Hill

SIMON & SCHUSTER
Rockefeller Center
1230 Avenue of the Americas
New York, New York 10020

10   9   8   7   6   5   4   3   2   1

Library of Congress Cataloging-in-Publication Data

Caras, Roger A.
   The cats of Thistle Hill : a mostly peaceable kingdom   / Roger A. Caras.
      p.   cm.
      1. Cats—Maryland—Anecdotes.   2. Animals—Maryland—
Anecdotes.   3. Caras, Roger A.—Homes and haunts—Maryland.   I. Title.
SF445.5C36   1994
636.8'009752—dc20   93-42775   CIP
ISBN: 0-671-75462-9

PHOTO CREDITS: Pages 16–17, 22, 25, 118–19, 182, 210, 216–17 by Mimi
Vang Olsen. All other photos by Dave and Jennifer McMichael.

ON THE TITLE PAGE: Xnard Takes the Sun. That's the old barn
behind him and in the left background is my study attached to the
kennel. Xnard would be at home anywhere. Now in his late teens,
he has learned how to accommodate himself to every opportunity
and get the world pretty much in shape his way. All in all, he is a
happy cat, and that is as it should be. He paid his dues early in
life and now is picking up the rewards.

This book is for Larry Hilford, who never got to visit the farm, and for Charlie Powell and George Carter, who did. Three fine men who loved animals each after his own fashion and who are gone much too early. I really hope there is a higher wisdom to explain it. And for Jill, the farmer's wife. And for Amanda.

Contents

Preface

MY LIFE, like any other life, has been a linear experience, a continuum. It started somewhere, *Nowhere,* and will eventually end at just about the same place, in all probability. Everything and everyone that has happened to that life between those two points are pretty much what that life has been all about, for although I dread sounding like a guru in the Himalayas, we are all reflecting pools. I am sure that, in one way or another, I owe a debt of gratitude to everyone I have ever known, recently and long ago, good and, in my estimation at least, awful. They all taught me something and some of them taught me a great deal. From some I learned self-defense. That was good, I needed it. Everybody does sooner or later. From others I learned the endless blessing of friendship. There was some true wisdom and some folly, love but never really hate (hate is far too expensive an emotional investment and I, at least, have never felt it was one I could afford), there were humor, warmth—a great deal of that—and, as the French say, *joie.* In that sense of debt, and gratitude probably too seldom articulated, my life has been unremarkable.

All of this applies equally, I am sure, to everybody else in the world. We are all collages, in a way, paste-ups, and although the details may appear to vary, the fabric is actually pretty much the same, although we are each unique. Oxymoronic though that may seem to be, I detect the glimmer of a truth there. It seems the more we differ the more alike we become. For all of that, the debt is the same. I am certain it can never be paid in full. So, thank you, Jill, Pamela, Clay, Joe, Sheila, Sarah, Joshua, Abaigeal, and Hannah. (You will be meeting them all again. They are the warp, but now on to the woof.)

There has been a second *faculty* in my life, another set of teachers and guides who have collectively had a tremendous influence on me. The members of this second group have had, for the most part, four feet each. They have been truly friends, largely. They have been tolerant, understanding, nonjudgmental, funny, sad, always close, and they have provided individual object lessons. Who are they? They are the Thistle Hill peaceable animal clan and their predecessors at other addresses. They have been the pets of my life.

We have a typical American home, you will agree as you read on. I am reasonably certain that during the course of writing this book we will become at least temporary hosts to yet other animals. If they settle in permanently or if they are here long enough to interact meaningfully with our current cast of characters, then they will be written in as well.

Unfortunately, there is always the possibility that a member of the cast will be gathered, so to speak. Every pet, unless it is a Galapagos tortoise, and what a terrible idea that would be, leaves sooner or later. One should always understand that. All of our pets here get regular veterinary care. (It takes four vets to cover the field.) Our pets get the best, appropriate nutrition. They are watched over and cared for and loved, but life does have to end for every creature above the single-cell level. The mind-set we use to get through those times that have happened to our family so often is that what is really important is that so-and-so lived, not that he or she died. One may grieve for a thirteen-year-old Bloodhound, as we did for Penny (she was born in our bedroom), but one really shouldn't wring one's hands, I believe, and wail, "Woe is me, why me, God?" For us, grieving has been a quiet, personal way of coming to grips with a necessary fact of life, and that is all death is.

But on to the living and the loving, after one essential observation. *Technically,* Jill and I are dog and cat breeders. In our thirty-nine years together we have produced exactly one litter of kittens and two litters of puppies. Maradadi, whose name meant "beautiful" in Swahili, a Silver-Ash Tabby, American Shorthair, was exquisite, and we thought about showing her. We had never shown cats and eventually did decide against it. Before that, however, we did cause Maradadi to be mated with an equally splendid tom from a very famous cattery, that of Richard Gebhardt in New Jersey, from whence Maradadi herself had originally come. Then we had her spayed.

Jill did show Bloodhounds and did produce exactly two litters in somewhat over twenty years. Carefully planned, they were adventures never to be repeated. All animals that come here are spayed or neutered except for most of the hoofed stock. Steakums, our Hereford steer, is, of course, but the horses are all mares and Maggie, our donkey, is a jenny. Our llama, Humboldt, and Huxley, our alpaca, are here on extended (permanent) breeding loans and can't be altered, obviously. Besides, the world is not overpopulated with llamas or alpacas. As for cats and dogs, there is rarely an excuse to maintain them intact. The oversupply is absolutely appalling, and as president of the ASPCA, I see the terrible results. Millions of animals are slaughtered every year for the want of homes. So, at Thistle Hill Farm surgery comes first, followed by a lifetime of loving care. The animals we have could never lead the lives described in this book unless they were spayed and neutered. The males would fight and wander, the females would be forever pregnant. If you, too, aspire to a peaceable kingdom (one animal or more), enlist the aid of your veterinarian early on. First comes surgery, then comes peace. It is a perfectly logical progression.

The House Down in the Hollow. Built in 1820, it was part of the Underground Railroad and is four-tenths of a mile south of the Mason-Dixon Line. The cats love the maple trees for the vantage points they provide.

16

1

The Farm

EVERY PLAY must have a set, every actor his stage, and every cat his secret. The animals that entwine their lives with ours and with each other's at Thistle Hill Farm do so in decidedly pleasant surroundings. It is really a complex community of wild and domestic animals. There are many tiers, many habitats, and marked seasonal shifts.

The farm was once called Lovely Plains and was awarded to one Isaac Dennis by the new federal government as a land grant in appreciation of his service against the British in the Revolutionary War. It was about a hundred and fifty acres then, but by the time we bought it (by then it was erroneously called Silver Run Farm, erroneous because the stream called Silver Run is actually on a nearby farm), it had been whittled down to thirty-five acres or thereabouts.

In this part of extreme northern Maryland, just four-tenths of a mile south of the Mason-Dixon line, the lending institutions accept unclosed surveys. There is no choice, since the original descriptions of the property date back to just after the turn of the century—the nineteenth century—and contain such tantalizing details as "if ye stand upon ye rock in the middle of ye stream and face ye elm tree to the east . . ." Since the stream referred to may have changed course in nearly two centuries, and the rock is probably gone, gobbled up into a foundation somewhere, and the elm tree surely long ago succumbed to blight, the modern surveyors can do little more than scratch their heads. A team of them spent a week here trying to determine what actually belongs to us and then gave up. The bank agreed. The Gentrys across the way told us when we first moved here that although it didn't make any difference to them our mailbox was on their farm. A further survey showed that not only is our mailbox on home turf, but a little of their woodland is on our farm. Who cares! We are all friends and share the same firm intent to preserve what is here. It simply is not true that you need fences in order to have good neighbors. What you need are good people.

At Thistle Hill Farm we have two streams (with an endless supply of wonderful wild watercress), seven pastures, two productive hay fields, and acres of very nice mixed woodlands with lots of dogwood and black walnut trees (one of the latter is about one hundred feet tall and has a drip line seventy feet across.) We have meadows, a really splendid marsh, and a spring that bubbles out of one of our hillsides. Wildflowers by the millions make the old place an ever-changing panorama. Its is rolling green horse country, and indeed, this is a horse farm.

Two hundred years of horse and dairy farming have made the soil rich beyond belief. Tomatoes cascade in an avalanche, and things like zucchini and cucumbers have to be picked very quickly or they become not only tasteless, but almost too large to carry. Melons, cucumbers, and the like that do get overlooked even for a few days have to be abandoned and in turn help make the soil even richer. We say hereabouts that you can go out and leave your door unlocked ten months of the year. In August and September it is best to lock up, though, or when you come home you will find your front hall full of an unidentified neighbor's zucchini. The ownership of squash can be difficult to trace, since they don't have blood, and, besides, squash abandonment isn't even a misdemeanor.

We have plenty of deer at Thistle Hill Farm, very

Good News. A quick check in the nesting box on the fencepost—we have bluebird eggs. Typically Thistle Hill Farm has three active bluebird nests throughout the season. We don't know how many species nest on the property, but it is a fair number including, happily, the ruby-throated hummingbird.

often out in the hay fields, sometimes in the marsh; skunks, raccoons, opossum occasionally, squirrel, chipmunks, cottontails, meadow mice, voles, fox, groundhogs, and a weasel family in, of all places, the middle of our most heavily used pasture, in a burrow under a bush.

We have a wonderful variety of birds, close to a couple of hundred species seasonally, I suppose. It is awesome when you think that in the world there are just over eight thousand species of birds and perhaps a couple of hundred of them reach this one farm! Of course, we are part of the great Atlantic Flyway.

Turkey vultures and red-tail hawks are in view every day. We have recorded red-shouldered and Swainson's hawks as well as rough-legged. We have had a bald eagle fly over twice lately and perhaps an immature one or two of the same species at other times. Peregrine falcons have passed through any number of times, migrants for certain. We have kestrels regularly and marsh hawks or harriers. We have seen a great horned owl heading for our woods once and a barn owl scanning our pastures for voles another time. We hear screech owls at night, and I am sure I have heard a barred owl, too, calling its characteristic, *"Who cooks for you."* Pheasants are all over the place sounding like huge, unoiled tin Siamese cats, and I believe I have seen grouse. Skeins of swans and of geese, Canada and snow, are seasonal, of course, and nine or ten species of ducks at least regularly beat overhead in their typically frantic way.

We named our little paradise Thistle Hill Farm because we have both hills and thistles to spare. The thistles mean goldfinches, and at times they seem as numerous as pigeons in Trafalgar Square. We have northern orioles; crows; bluebirds nesting along our fence lines in houses we provide; very fat cardinals; indigo buntings; catbirds; mockingbirds; swallows nesting everywhere but in our living room, it seems; grosbeaks; doves; martins; pewees; phoebes; flycatchers; horned larks; blue jays; gray jays; snow buntings, seasonally; downy, hairy, red-headed and red-bellied woodpeckers; flickers; sapsuckers; kingbirds; ruby-throated hummingbirds (and lots of sphinx moths to imitate them); sparrows and flinches and all the rest. Our neigh-

Mary Todd Lincoln and a Favorite Haunt of All the Cats—the Woodpile. All kinds of wonderful things are to be found there—hopefully not another copperhead.

bors the Gentrys at Weathered Wood Farm have a pond, and we regularly see great blue heron coming and going. Cattle egrets stop off here. It is a lovely mix richly accented by a splendid variety of butterflies. (We have planted a large number of butterfly bushes to help that facet of our wonderland expand. It works like a champ.)

Although Jill doesn't like them (I do!), we have a nice variety of snakes: milk snakes, corn snakes, black racers, hognose snakes, garter snakes, ringnecks, grass snakes; all have their place. We caught a copperhead in the driveway last year, and I drove him two miles down the road to turn him loose on an old stone wall that is now part of a woodland. Why not? A few farms from here the farmer got bitten by a rattlesnake two years ago, so I have to suppose we may get them, too. I have never heard one or seen one. If one turns up, and I can get at him, down the road he goes, too. Venomous snakes can be a worry with grandchildren and animals, but they certainly shouldn't be executed, just moved.

Bats live in our barn, quivering blankets of them, and so do an unfortunate number of pigeons and starlings. I should shoot the birds to keep our hay clean, so our vets say, but I really don't want to do that. I steeled myself to the task one day, loaded a twenty-two up with dust shot, and headed into the loft. I didn't fire a shot, but I did come away feeling guilty for being willing to do it, almost. My son, Clay, and son-in-law, Joe, go up from time to time and contour the population curve somewhat. Neither is a hunter, but they are a little more realistic than I am. It really isn't fair to livestock to feed hay that has been constantly subjected to a rain of bird droppings. There are lots of aspects of keeping livestock properly, any animals in fact, that may not be aesthetically pleasing. I am sure that is very true if you are raising animals for food. That is something we have never done. How can you eat someone you know, for heaven's sakes?

The main house at Thistle Hill, then Lovely Plains, was built in 1820 and has walls about eighteen inches thick. One exposed wall in the entryway shows its original construction: chink and chestnut log. The beams in the lower of three living rooms are exposed, and the engineers have pointed out that they were salvaged for use when the house was built. They probably came from an eighteenth-century barn or perhaps even a barge that brought bulk cargo down a river nearby. Once there was a railroad near here and a paper mill, but both are long gone.

The area where we are located is called Pretty Boy for the Pretty Boy Reservoir not far from here. That names comes from a stallion who fell into the reservoir when it was under construction and drowned. Such was his name. We shop in the Pretty Boy Market and vote at the Pretty Boy Elementary School. His influence is all over this area. Pretty Boy must have been quite a horse.

The barn, like the house, is built into the side of a hill and is called a bank barn, typical for these parts. The stable is entered on one level and the hay and vehicle area on another, on the opposite side. It is huge and is all chestnut and oak. The rafters above the hay are stacked with fifteen-foot chestnut trunks slabbed on two sides. They were cut and never used, just stored. They are quite rare and valuable now, and I bartered some for some work on the driveway a while back.

The house, like most of the old houses in this area, is built down in a hollow at the foot of a hill. Logic would suggest that weather was the main consideration, but the local story has it that houses were situated that way to avoid attracting the attention of witches. We have been here over five years now and indeed not a witch have we seen. And with all these familiars you

The Old Oak and Chestnut Barn. It was built before 1850, years after the farm was laid out and the house built. We assume there was another barn before this one, but in the same spot? Or is there a foundation we haven't discovered yet? The Barn is in the process of being restored. The near corner of the foundation has just been taken out and rebuilt. The lower level has been black-topped for easier cleaning. The bad planks will soon be replaced.

The Road into and out of Thistle Hill Farm. It is a road to peace and the good life for all who are good and peaceful. Except for routine visits to the veterinarian, no animal has to leave once it has settled in.

would think we would have seen at least one. Whatever works.

The house, which is on three main levels, has grown over the years into a kind of wonderful rambling affair with many bedrooms and bathrooms, three sitting rooms, a library, large formal dining room, large country eat-in kitchen, and even a secret fourth-level hideout leading north toward Pennsylvania by tunnel.

We assume the hideout was a last depot in the underground railroad, but that still requires researching. I know two people who were down there, before its entrance was blocked to keep kids out, and each claims a totally different scenario as to what is or was there. Since both men are known to be deeply devoted to pathological lies, and they agree on not one single detail, the matter can rest for the moment and perhaps some day we will have it excavated. The more imaginative of the two stories includes a coffin down there and in it the unoccupied uniform of a Confederate officer, his sword and pistol wrapped in oily rags and still in good condition. We are approximately thirty-five miles south-east of Gettysburg, and I am sure old buildings all around here contain that kind of secret. Whether Thistle Hill Farm does or not we don't know. The other story describes an empty room with a single child's spur on the dirt floor. One thing, if we uncorked that chamber and its tunnel our cats could get into trouble. I wonder how many cats have died in deteriorating underground structures of one kind or another. It would be a shame to turn a tunnel whose original intent was mercy and

Jean Valjean Has a Truly Cute Face. He is in fact a handsome cat and as of this writing is showing signs of following Omari's lead. He may soon be a house cat. He is fine with dogs and other cats and may one day forgive us our size, certainly, and perhaps our smell. His original skittishness has all but disappeared. At times he lets people pick him up and hold him. When we met him he nearly wiped Jill out for trying that— stitches, rabies shots, the whole nine yards.

freedom into a dungeon of horrors. We don't know, by the way, that that hasn't already happened. The presumed tunnel has already collapsed in two places after torrential rains, and we had those exposed portions filled in. We had volunteers willing to go try to see what was down there, but I refused permission. I have the liability insurance but not the heart for that kind of thing.

Besides the house and the barn there is my study, which consists of four rooms and is attached to a kennel. Another building, an old shed from late in the last century, had an electrical fire last year and burned right to its stone foundation. We buried the debris and have turned the foundation into a kind of secret rose garden. The shed may have once been a chicken house, or perhaps it had goats, too. It did have a ramp as well as two doors. We'll never know now. The fire was so hot that glass jars full of nails melted into solid clumps of glass and metal.

A guest cottage is under construction so that guests who are allergic to cats and dogs can still stay over. There is a pool house, and a heated pool, too, and that completes in outline form the architectural features of Thistle Hill Farm. Combining the nooks and crannies in the big old barn, the endless tunnels and nests in the hay we store there—hundreds of bales at a time—and all of the secret places in the woods and near the streams, there are many, many thousands of places for cats to hide, hunt, do whatever they want to do except, of course, reproduce. It is a cat's paradise especially, since all but two, Cosette and her son Jean, have access to the house, too. And those two hooligans have the barn.

Cosette's son, all black and jowly, JEAN VALJEAN came with the barn. He would like to be friends, and we accommodate that wish in every way possible. Jill did pick him up once, but she had to have stitches and rabies shots. She didn't want to have him put down so she did the rabies course instead. So far, at least, Jean has been unable to cross the barrier the way Omari, another wild cat, did. He does let Karen pet him, but then, Karen could get a response from a rattlesnake.

COSETTE, Jean Valjean's mother, has moved closer to the barrier than her son has and has been inside the house a couple of times and even sat in Jill's lap for a few minutes. But the barn is still her thing. She purrs and does figure eights around your ankles, but skitters away if you reach down and try to touch her. Talk about ambivalence! They are happy, though, and cared for in the necessary ways.

What do the cats do with the whole world of a farm to explore? That, in large measure, is what this book is all about—scheduling. Cats no less than dogs, and perhaps in many cases more so, have places to go and things to do. It may all appear to be casual and without form or purpose to us—in fact it most often does seem that way—but it is not that way for the cats themselves, I am sure. Depending on the weather and how much time they spend outside, they have serious rounds to make. At least, after watching them and fol-

lowing them whenever it has been possible, I am convinced that they do what they do with real purpose, and
rarely do two do anything the same way at all.

There is a common misconception about cats in
general that we should clear up before getting on with
the Thistle Hill Farm cats in particular. It is often held
that we have given everything to the cat and expected
nothing of it in return. That is patently not true. Somewhat over four thousand years ago, when the Egyptians
began the intricate process of domestication, using the
small African wildcat found along the Nile as raw material, they made demands of the cat that were directly
contrary to the beast's nature. The only social species of
cat in the world is the African lion, and that four- to
five-hundred-pound giant didn't figure in the formation
of our pets at all. The African wildcat that did was and
still is fiercely independent, and except when a male and
a female associate briefly to breed and when a mother is
with kittens to raise and educate, they are solitary.

There are reasons why all but one wild feline species are solitary. Breeding opportunities can be enhanced
by secure territorial claims, and a prey base can best be
exploited without having to worry about and perhaps
drive off competition. The lion is the exception because
it hunts most often among vast herds, millions of hoofed
animals endlessly migrating along fixed routes. Most
other cats rely on a less dependable food supply and
generally hunt under conditions where it is serendipity
or die. Cats virtually always do better alone and have

evolved to live that way, all but the African and the almost extinct Asian lion.

A species that goes for millennia without existing in a social unit evolves lacking the desire or skills to deal with social situations. Cats resent other cats and do not have the dog's natural desire to please, accept, share, or give ground to other animals of their own kind whom they can only perceive as competitors. But the Egyptians and all cat owners who have followed their four-millennia-old lead have said to the cat: *"No good. You simply have to fit in. You have to become in every sense communal. Do what dogs do, although you have no genetic tradition for pack etiquette. Forget your inherited behavioral traits; do it our way."* And so cats have given in. Although there are exceptions (generally only because they were not conditioned early enough), most cats do, however unwillingly, become social when it is required of them. It goes against their grain, but they have been willing to make the big swap.

Many of the stories and accounts that follow demonstrate two things—how difficult it can be for a cat to deny tens of millions of years of evolution (the last four thousand years camping out near our hearth are as nothing by comparison), and how cats are willing to try to accommodate us and our style despite that historical tug and pull. It is a constant battle for many of them, and sometimes they appear to lose on both counts.

Omari Thinks Things Over. He was once nearly euthan-
ized, he was so wild and unmanageable. He has chosen
another lifestyle now and is one of the world's nicest
cats. Why or how he made the 180-degree turn is a
mystery. He remains very introspective at times and
rests in the shade, perhaps contemplating his own wisdom, one that literally saved his life.

2

The Story of Omari

OMARI IS one of the strangest cats I have ever known, and after turning an amazing number of sharp, unpredictable corners in life, any one of which could have thrown a lesser cat, he now leads a somewhat bizarre private life. Only he knows what it all means. A cat, like a human being, is surrounded at all times by a ring of positive and negative incentives. It is impossible to analyze them from the outside looking in and know what might tip the balance from moment to moment. The directions life takes depend on the relative values of those pluses and minuses, but how could we possibly judge what they might be even for another of our own species, much less for a member of another?

Our first word of the tiny marmalade-and-white tomcat trapped at the stable in Bridgehampton, New York, came from local volunteer rescue people. They are the people who in so many of our communities do all of the work saving animals, fostering them, and finding them new homes, often spending their own money on the veterinary care that is needed along the way. They are saints without haloes. In our community then it was ARF, the Animal Rescue Fund of the Hamptons.

A feral queen had been allowed to bear her un-wanted litter in the hay and straw barn at the stable. The size of the litter was unknown, but the kittens were by then large enough so that the stable operator was shooting them whenever he saw one long enough to get a shot in with his trusty .22. The mother was truly wild and could not be handled, and neither could her offspring. They were small, wild cats, all teeth and claws and wild, raging sounds. The humane workers had trapped two of them and wanted us to take on one of them "as a challenge." They had another patsy lined up for the other.

Via the surgical theater at the local veterinary hospital, Omari came to us in a carrier that he had all but totally destroyed. When we picked him up at the hospital the vet-tech wished us "Good luck!" in a voice I felt was a little too dramatic. In fact it was sardonic and insensitive. I never have liked that we-who-are-about-to-die-salute-you tone of voice.

At home, we put Omari through an established coming-on-board routine. Jill had stacked a couple of old kitchen cabinets in the laundry room to form a good approximation of a feline apartment house. Scraps of carpeting made each unit comfortable. There were food and water dishes and a fresh litter box. Omari the unhandleable would spend seven to ten days locked in, while the earth's magnetic field surrounding our home territory imprinted on him like a giant fingerprint. By then it should be his home territory as well, and he would be able to home to it. That was the object, to create a center to his universe. I firmly believe the earth's magnetic fields (they can be mapped) automatically provide that focus for our pets as they do for migrating birds, fish, and insects.

We lived then on a quiet county road, and the house was set well back among an acre of trees leading down to our own beach. We would eventually open the laundry-room window, and Omari would be an inside-outside cat. That lifestyle is feasible only in a setting with very little traffic, never in a home hard by a road, and only with animals that have been spayed or neutered and are without the urge to wander. They are then far less likely to get into a serious fight.

Eight days or so passed, and although Omari quickly adjusted to food and water being brought into his benevolent dungeon there was no question of his

being touched. If you even thought about it, he was gone—behind the water heaters, behind the furnace, behind the dryer. He was a very spooky little cat. But the time was upon us, and the Prisoner of Zenda was about to see sunlight. The window was opened, and we went outside to see if Omari would emerge. In about twenty minutes he did. He had apparently been hanging back working up his nerve, and when he came out it was for real, like a ball bearing from a slingshot, into the bushes and away.

That was at about eight o'clock in the morning. By three o'clock Omari was back hanging around outside the laundry window. By five he was inside gobbling up

Omari Typically in a Hurry. Omari, whether he is collecting sticks or horse manure or snuggling up for a good scratch and purr session, never does things by halves. Heading down the hill past the barn toward the house, he is purposeful and driven by inner resources of strength and determination. He leads a busy life and likes it that way. Thistle Hill suits him fine. He has his niche all figured out and fits his life like a glove.

the fresh food that had been left for him. He was locked in for the night because he was still quite small, and we had, there in East Hampton, New York, both foxes and a variety of owls including a great horned raider of the night with a nest nearby. For a great horned owl a kitten would be a piece of cake, approximately literally.

That became the routine—come and go ad lib— and eventually we just accepted it as a done deal, the way Omari himself did, I am sure. He began to mix with our other cats in the garden and even learned to ignore our dogs. Jill managed to pick him up a few times briefly, and once or twice he even purred. But he was still a wild thing.

Then one day Omari was gone. It must have been two weeks or perhaps a little longer than that before we saw him again. Then there he was, back to the old routine. He seemed a little wilder than before his sojourn, or at least less anxious to interact.

And that is the way Omari grew up in East Hampton. He grew to be a very large, burly cat. He wanted his privacy, and except when we had to trap him so that he could be altered and get boosters for his shots, we didn't handle him. At the size he grew to be he could have done a lot of damage if an attempt had been made to restrain him. He periodically vanished for anywhere from one day to two weeks, but he continued to flourish. He was obviously as neat as a pin about himself. He never made a litter-box mistake in his stronghold, and his coat was always clean and glistening, with the white areas as white as could be.

We made the decision to leave the Atlantic Ocean and our waterfront home in East Hampton behind in 1988 after twenty-five years. We had found what was about to become Thistle Hill Farm. Serendipity had struck again. Now, what on earth were we to do with Omari? No one in East Hampton wanted him. Only we could possibly consider him a rewarding pet and even for us it was stretching the truth. Could he adjust, would he adjust, should we ask him to? It wasn't a situation that could be left to resolve itself. Either he went with us or we had him put to sleep; there were no alternatives. Just leaving him behind was out of the question. No pet ever deserves to be abandoned. There is simply no excuse for it, although it is something that happens in this country millions of times a year.

I had half decided that making the big move was more than we could expect of Omari or he of us. We had no setup ready at Thistle Hill. There were many other animals to provide for and a large house and large apartment to consolidate into a single residence. We didn't know the turf we were moving on to. It seemed a perfectly lethal muddle, and then one morning Jill signaled me to come over to the window. The matter resolved itself. There was Omari, glistening orange and white, taking the morning sun in a birdbath in our garden. He was positively golden. He was young, handsome, and obviously very healthy. No problem; there were already at least three barn cats at Thistle Hill, and they were probably as wild as Omari was. Whatever the outcome, Omari was moving south of the Mason-Dixon line. Initially he wouldn't like the physical part of it, but we weren't asking for volunteers. (Pets, after all, generally have little say in these matters.) At least he would be alive. I don't think we ever would have found it in our hearts to go through with his execution under any circumstances, but it had to be considered. But now that we had given death its due, it was time to get on with life. All members of the Caras zoo would survive the move in fine form.

Moving Omari proved more difficult than anticipated. Three different times he was caught and pushed, snarling and yowling, into a travel case. How he hates any form of restraint! He was insane with fear and rage, and we were afraid he would hurt himself thrashing around in the case like a creature possessed. The effect of between five or six hours of that racket on the nerves of the designated driver was unthinkable for man or beast. So the necessary was done. Omari was drugged on instructions of our veterinarian, and he made the trip blissfully unaware of anything. He did have a terrible hangover when he awoke in Maryland. He had no idea of where he was or how he got there.

In stages, one just slightly more agonizing than another, the big switch took place. For Omari and the other cats it was the old, familiar routine. One to two weeks of confinement in the laundry room, then slow release to explore outside with all food and water dishes kept inside. Ten of our then eleven cats fell into line, and all of them were back at dusk their first time out— all of them but Omari. He vanished the first time he got his paw outside the door. He had been waiting.

We knew only a fraction of our own territory at that early stage, and we had no idea where to even begin to look. Omari didn't seem to be around the barn; he didn't appear with the three barn cats (Cosette, her son Jean Valjean, and his sister, who was not to live long enough to be given a name). We could see much of our beautiful marsh from our windows, but we saw not a sign of the elusive Omari. Apparently, he was not to survive the move after all, despite all the effort.

Thistle Hill Farm is set in a "belt" that runs along the state line between Pennsylvania and Maryland—the Mason-Dixon line, in fact. It is locally called the "Hereford Belt" and for some reason it is hit by heavier winds, rain, and snow than areas immediately north and south of it. We don't see that as a problem; the weather just can be a little more stimulating here than in the next valley. No one in the area would miss the odd tornado, of course, but the electric utility people usually get the power back on pretty quickly—and we use gas for cooking.

One night we were getting a wind- and rainstorm that was for the record book. It was really blowing up, and it was branch-against-roof-and-windowpane time. I went to the rear door to make sure there was no one shut out in the fury, and as soon as I opened the door, in shot Omari, looking as if he had had to swim Chesapeake Bay to get home. He jumped up next to Jill, who was sitting on a banquette in the kitchen, and began to purr. From that moment, the first time we had seen the wild creature in twelve weeks, to this, Omari has been a homebody and one of the sweetest of all our cats. He is a lap-sitter, a cuddler, a head-butter, and he's in just about every night of the year. If it is really very warm he may spend the night on the porch, but most often he is inside looking for a vacant lap he can stake out. The only vestige of his former look-but-don't-touch self is he doesn't like being hugged. He prefers to come to us rather than to be scooped off his feet and squished. (Jill is a squisher.)

If we try to read or play Scrabble and ignore Omari, forget it. There he is, marching back and forth with his tail straight up in the air inviting us to smell his anus in greeting. None of us is really into that, and Omari tolerates our lack of etiquette and settles for a good scratching around the ears. He is so large now that it can be absolutely suffocating to have him on your lap. He seems to understand and settles in against your thigh, holding his bosom on with his thick front legs.

Are we absolutely certain this is Omari and that he really did undergo the transformation? After all, three months is a long time. We are absolutely certain, and if we could be wrong (doubtful in this case) our animals could not be—*that is not possible.* They all knew him, and he knew them. How do we know that? They ignored each other. Imagine a twenty-pound cat marching in on your pets without having its scent on file with them. At the absolute minimum you would see curiosity, at the worst blood and flying fur. It is not possible for anything as intriguing as the smell of a new cat or dog on turf not to arouse at least the interest of the regulars. No doubt! It was Omari who walked out of here in one mode and walked back in three months later in a totally different one, one from which he has not varied in the almost four years since.

Omari did have one serious setback. What is now my office and the kennels was formerly a stallion barn. The stalls do not share common walls, but each is sheathed in very heavy planking, heavy enough to withstand the punishment an excited stud Thoroughbred can mete out when there is a mare in heat on the grounds. One day Omari vanished again. We figured he was off on another of his marathon walkabouts and didn't expect to see him again soon. What would he be like when he came back this time, if he came back?

On about the third day the workmen who were converting the old stallion barn into its present configuration heard a pitiful mewing and came to get us. It didn't take long to locate the origin of the sound. We had not realized that the adjacent stall walls, only inches apart, were not capped. Neither, evidently, did Omari. He had jumped up on a wall and slipped down between them. There he was like a pancake pinned between stalls number three and four. Carefully, the workmen skinned off one heavy sheathing of stallionproof planks and Omari, thoroughly displeased with his most recent adventure, covered with cobwebs and sawdust, was lifted out. For a creature who so despises restraint it must have been a terrible couple of days and nights. He got a special dinner that night—the food of foods for dogs as well as cats: liver.

Omari's misadventure in the stallion barn highlights a terrible fact of feline life. Cats are curious and that can be lethal. When a cat disappears, besides creating a terrible sense of loss, it leaves the owners with that dreadful feeling of not knowing. Have curious cats vanished into the tunnel that leads out from our secret basement? Cosette's daughter died during her explorations in the barn where she was born. She had littermates that vanished before we even moved here. A farm is one of the best of all possible worlds for cats and one of the most dangerous. There is so much to explore, so many places to snoop around, and so many places like the stallion barn, where a misstep can lead to a slow death. Omari survived that time because we weren't in Africa or someplace else where we go regularly and because there were workers on the job there. He was one lucky cat.

Omari has remained a homebody to this day. Although he is an inside-outside cat, he comes back every evening. I think he has probably had enough high adventure in his life. We have discovered part of his routine although, of course, he still has secrets. Up until 1988 this house got its water from undoubtedly the same source used by the first inhabitants in the early 1800s. There is a stream bubbling out of the side of a hill only a couple of dozen feet to the west of the house, one of two streams that feed the marsh behind the house. Sometime, probably before the turn of this century, the mouth of the stream where it emerged from the hill and became surface water was enclosed in a small cement blockhouse. It is very well hidden back under a thick, literally impenetrable growth of heavily armed briars. For a man to get in there would require a machete or other cutting tool—a heavy-duty one.

Just before we bought Thistle Hill Farm the state of Maryland passed a law that says a residence cannot be legally transferred for occupancy unless it has a well. No more surface water for human consumption is allowed. So we drilled a deep well with a submerged pump, had the new water source tested and approved, and complied. But the old stream still bubbles away and is perfectly potable so we still pump it to the barn for the livestock. In his travels Omari found his way back through the brambles and has a post on top of the small blockhouse. I was suspicious when I saw him coming and going into that particular thick growth and got close enough on several occasions to see him on his perch, staring downstream and looking very contented, soothed perhaps by the sound and perhaps by the rumbling feeling of the water coming out of the hillside behind him and tumbling through the cement container below him. That is one of his stop-offs. I believe it is a daily one, usually visited earlier in the day.

The marsh behind the house is curved around the edge of the woods on the far side and, except in summer when the growth is as tall as a man and as thick as a lion's mane, much of it is in view. At least twice a day Omari can be seen from the house picking his way along the far edge or, as he is now as I write this, sitting on the near edge, on high ground just behind the house. He moves gingerly, careful where he steps, and I think that is a function of his not wanting to get his feet wet.

Occasionally Omari visits a clump of extremely thick growth about fifty feet from the house, at the opposite end of the house from the stream's blockhouse. It is so thick it cannot be penetrated by any of us, but we know a spring surfaces there briefly. It could be the only explanation for the growth that encloses it. Omari goes there, too. He seems to have a thing about water. He has never been seen going in it and is virtually always dry and neat, but he likes being close to water and its sources.

Omari working the edge of a marsh every day, Omari in his secret jungles every day at either end of the house, and, keep in mind, he is always alone. He gets along perfectly well with all of our dogs and cats, whether he is inside or out, but his work is solitary. An obvious conclusion could be that Omari is a great hunter who stalks his hunting block like a Bengal tiger and kills almost at will. The amazing thing is that this large, once-wild cat is not a hunter at all. He has found a strange substitute activity. First, though, how do we know he is not a hunter?

When we are out on the lawn, on the front porch, or out by the pool the tranquillity is periodically shattered by shrill shouting and a sudden explosion of activity. Somebody has seen something with something else in its mouth. Chipmunks, mice, voles, birds, snakes, all get caught, and the rescue missions are successful often enough to encourage the mad running around that ensues every time there is an impending kill. Our dogs are seldom if ever involved. Just about every one of our cats except Omari is, fairly regularly. We have never caught Omari with an animal victim. At times the shouting and arm waving will catch one of the other cats so by surprise that it will drop its prey. On a number of occasions we have seen that prey shoot right by Omari as he turned his head to watch it escape. To our certain knowledge, he has not pounced, when it would have been easy for him to do so.

On scores of occasions, on the other hand, we have seen Omari coming up to the back porch with a suspicious dark form in his mouth. Early on, after his miraculous transforming *walkabout,* as Jill calls it, we descended on him only to find his substitute secret. He is a retrieving cat. Every day, excepting only those days when the weather makes the job impossible, Omari, often looking for all the world like George Burns with his cigar, brings us sticks. They average one to six inches in length and are usually between half an inch and an inch in diameter. He brings them to near the back door, drops them off, and heads out on the search for others. It is quaint or something like that, but it is also a bit of a nuisance, since Omari brings us so many sticks that they have become a slipping hazard on the pathway. They have to be swept up and carted off. There can be three or four dozen at a time, sometimes more than that. Scattered among the sticks will be the occasional chunk of horse manure. That means some of Omari's scavenging swings take him into the paddock, perhaps into the barn. I often wonder whether a bit of horse manure delivered to the back door is a special offering and what significance it has.

In fact, what significance does any of this behavior have? Perhaps nothing more than that it is Omari's "thing." Each day he makes his rounds, and instead of doing a very catlike thing, such as murdering everything in sight, he collects mountains of cigarlike offerings and delivers them to our back and to a lesser extent our front door.

Cats that do hunt very often leave things like whole voles and mouseless tails and whiskers on bed pillows; that is fairly typical country-cat behavior. I have heard these generally unwelcome artifacts variously described as *love tributes* and *boasting*. Frankly, I haven't the foggiest notion what they are, once the anthropomorphism is whittled back. I am not at all certain what we are looking at. Perhaps it harks back to adults bringing food to the lair to feed cubs or kittens. If that is the case, our cats really have things turned around. We are supposed to be the nurturers.

Whatever it means, however it happened, Omari, a Thistle Hill Regular, stalks the edges of a marsh, walks the edges of a wood, visits two very hidden, very secret jungle hideouts, stalks a paddock area, and finds cigar-butt-sized treasures by the gross to carry back to the house and leave, I guess for us to enjoy. Even if I don't know what he is doing I am happy that he is happy and that he came to live with us here at Thistle Hill Farm and find himself at last, sticks and all. The sticks are, after all, a harmless vice even if Omari is addicted to them. One thing is certain: between the horses and the woods we are never going to run out of offerings for Omari to bring home.

Omari's Offerings. The back porch has to be swept and mopped down yet again! Three times a day is not an unusual count. It took Omari about two hours to locate sticks "good enough" to bring as offerings to the back door, not to mention the nasty bits of fresh horse manure. Moles, voles, and mice I could understand, but why wood and poop?

Teddy Looking for an Insult and Expecting One. Always alert and suspicious when it comes to other animals, Teddy, Thistle Hill's only fighter, is gentle and trusting with humans, even complete strangers. His distrust of his fellow critters was apparently born during his six months as a street person in San Francisco after he escaped en route to the SFSPCA. Who knows what went before that? Slowly, thanks first to Emmy and later to Marmalade, Martha Custis Washington, and Mary Todd Lincoln, he is getting better—slowly.

3

Teddy's Tale

TEDDY COULD BECOME an American icon. His is a real-life saga. He is a legend-type cat, a living folk song, although no one has yet sat down to write the banjo and guitar music appropriate to his tale. Teddy is the stuff of folklore. Teddy is a soap opera. If there is a great cat in the sky he probably looks at least a little like Teddy, or he would like to. He came to us a Damien. It didn't suit. Since he has certain teddy-bear qualities he got his new, much more suitable, name.

As far as we know Teddy originated in the vicinity of San Francisco; at least it was in the Queen of American Cities that we found him (which shows good taste on his part). We were visiting the wonderful San Francisco Society for the Prevention of Cruelty to Animals (SFSPCA), and Jill spotted this oversized, somewhat too dark, certainly overage and well-used neutered Seal-Point Siamese tom. There is not a great deal of logic to adopting a shelter cat in California when you live in Maryland, but as a character on the Jack Benny radio show back in the 1940s used to say, *"If you look, you'll see; if you like, you'll buy."* Jill looked, she saw, she liked, and Teddy went into the hold of our 747 for the trip back to Baltimore. Who needs logic? And besides, the SFSPCA executive director, Rich Avanzino, egged Jill on behind my back.

All we knew of his history was that someone unknown was in the process of bringing him to the SFSPCA to turn him in when, just outside the shelter door, he wriggled out of his carrier and escaped into the maze of industrial buildings in the area. For six months the SFSPCA tried to trap him, and at last they were successful. Teddy was checked over by a veterinarian and declared to be "OK, if somewhat used," and he was certainly that. He was a well-scarred, fat-faced old tom of heroic, even Falstaffian, proportions and was obviously considerably older than the "5 years plus" notation on his documents suggested. But he was and is a great purrer, one of the greatest of our time, and he has a certain comfortable bulk to him. He does, though, have no center of gravity, and picking him up is like trying to hoist a well-greased, half-filled water mattress onto a towel rack.

What his records didn't show was that those early years in the port of San Francisco had allowed him to move only halfway across the bridge toward the human lifestyle dictate. He is an all-out card-carrying people lover, but he immediately made it clear that that was as far as he would go—one species. All four-legged types were out. At the sight of another cat or dog, however benign the other animal's intent, Teddy went ballistic. The first time a Greyhound came yowling down the hall wearing Teddy, all of him, like a snood, spitting and snarling, we knew we would have to address the matter sooner rather than later.

Fortunately, the main house at Thistle Hill Farm has three ample living rooms, and it was possible to lock one off just for big, old, tough Teddy alone. It has a great antique English oak door with a frosted glass pane that carries the quaint legend H. BABB BUILDER AND UNDERTAKER. It also had a heavy brass hook and eye so Teddy could be kept from chance encounters. He had become the prisoner in the tower. At least, we could console ourselves, his isolation was self-imposed. It was not the way we would prefer it.

There are a number of places in the house where we can hook up VCRs and enjoy the art and history of film, but we inevitably chose what became known as

Teddy's room, to give him as much company as we could. Many a fine film have we watched with that badly stuffed pillow of a cat smothering one lap or another and purring up a storm. An important architectural detail: because the carpeting is thick at the portal to Teddy's room, there is no sill installed under the door, but there is space, an inch or so. That is important to remember.

Now we must leave Teddy alone in his tower in order to introduce the next character to play a key role in his tale. Up in coastal Connecticut a rather pretty tortoiseshell cat my grandson, Joshua, would eventually name Emmy, was working over a neighborhood trying to decide on her next home, even as Teddy was defining

Emmy on the Lawn. Before she went house hunting in New London, Connecticut, and chose our son's family, Emmy didn't even know that Thistle Hill Farm or Maryland, for that matter, existed. Now it is her turf, and whatever her pre-Caras history may have been, it is forever unknowable. She has surely forgotten it, and we can't learn it. That is one of the mysteries of cats. Who are they, really, what have they seen, what, indeed, have they survived?

the terms of his world in Maryland. What her life before had been we can't even speculate. We would come to know that neither dogs nor other cats bothered her in the slightest. She hears celestial music, I am sure. She has proven to be a very self-assured young queen, very pulled together, definitely a NOW cat. If cats think about such things, Emmy is a feminist and quite properly so.

On several occasions during her selection trials the little queen stopped off at the home of our physician son, Clay, his wife, and their two children. Despite the fact that daughter-in-law Sheila is seriously allergic to cats, Emmy-to-be was allowed in, fed, and invited to bed down for the night. Joshua and his younger sister, Abaigeal, were delighted with the little, cuddly stranger who always arrived at dusk. The Emmy business only became serious when her drop-in frequency rate increased enough to make it clear that she had made her choice. She would be yet another Caras cat, Connecticut Chapter. But Sheila was still coughing and wheezing. The obvious solution—Emmy would come to Maryland and always be here at Thistle Hill Farm for Joshua and Abaigeal when they came to visit.

All of that was pretty routine, and sauntering, self-possessed, easygoing Emmy had her surgery, then her shots, and settled in as a Regular. She began exploring at once, of course, and quickly discovered the door to Teddy's dungeon. It seemed to fascinate her. She just had to find out who the beguiling stranger was behind the great oak door. What were we hiding, what was in the family closet? We often found her in the hall outside the H. BABB door gazing at it unblinkingly. She hunkered down and stared as if she thought she could eventually burn a hole through it.

One day I was going into our bedroom and had to pass close to the door to Teddy's lockup. Emmy was lying on her back on our side of the door with one paw stretched out as far as it could go. She was reaching under the H. BABB door! I got down and peered along Emmy's arm. She and Teddy were holding paws. With Jill standing by in case we had to separate one cat from the other surgically, I opened the door. With such supreme confidence that it suggested a prior agreement,

Emmy strode into Teddy's chamber. He just watched her as we watched them. She ignored him and investigated the room she had never visited before. He watched and then slowly, almost hesitantly, walked over to her. She rolled over on her side and then her back, and he began to bathe her. It was as simple as that. When in doubt, try a little of that good old social-grooming stuff. Teddy was not a cat without a soul after all. He was more than just a thunderous purr. He was, in truth, all heart.

So Teddy the Solitary gained a companion. Each day we would find Emmy outside his door, sometimes holding paws with Teddy under the door, sometimes just rubbing against the door, purring. Sometimes Emmy would spend the night with Teddy, but every day, one way or another, they spent hours together. Emmy had developed other imperatives of her own both inside the house and out on the farm, but she always found time for a visit with the dark stranger in the tower. And when Emmy arrived, there was rubbing and bathing. They often slept rolled up together on either the couch or an old oak doll's bed they both seemed to favor. Several of the dozens of teddy bears that live all over this house are always perched at one end of the bed watching over them, Teddy and his visiting mistress, Emmy. (The teddy bears are in almost every room of the house, but they do come together once a year. On Boxing Day—the day after Christmas—all the teddy bears assemble, and our grandchildren, each by written invitation, join in the Teddy Bears' Tea Party. The children are expected to dress for the event. The bears come as they are.)

Is that it, then? An unknown beginning, the attempted turn-in at the SFSPCA, the escape, evasion of capture for six months, the flight across America, the initial shock of the Thistle Hill population, solitary confinement, the burgeoning love affair with Emmy that began through an inch and a half of solid oak? Is that how the story closes? By no means. That is how it begins. Teddy has apparently no end of secret dimensions.

The next stage of the saga was shaping up in nearby rural Pennsylvania. Faithful Karen Dorn, farm manager here at Thistle Hill, brought us, in rapid succession, our three youngest cats: Martha Custis Washington, without a tail, and Mary Todd Lincoln and Marmalade, both with tails.

MARMALADE was abandoned with two littermates beside a country road in southern Pennsylvania. They were much too young to survive. I have never figured out what people say to themselves when they do that. Marmalade, an orange tabby, was generally in good shape and obviously socialized, so one can conjecture that she was handled a good deal if not loved before being abandoned to die. She hasn't really gotten over the shock of whatever it was that happened. She may be suspicious the rest of her life. You never know. Cats are not always ready or perhaps able to set aside the baggage they arrive with. If they have to live with it, so do the people who take them on. Cats are not neurotic by

The Face of Martha Custis Washington, One of Teddy's "Kids." She is an introspective little thing, yet she is interactive and an industrial-strength purrer. She hangs out with Teddy and his other two foster kittens. She still tries to nurse on her single-parent father and he lets her although she is full grown. It is a bit weird, but they are happy.

choice any more than people are. They are forgiving and we must be, too. Fair is fair.

MARY TODD LINCOLN is gray and pinky white. She is a very sweet little cat with a huge purr. When she really gets going she sounds like James Earl Jones doing a voice-over. She is just one more case of inexplicable abandonment in nearby Pennsylvania, in an area we know as Pennsyltucky. She is very people-oriented.

MARTHA CUSTIS WASHINGTON is pretty and pleasantly meddlesome, a gray job that someone didn't want. Our records are not perfect so we don't know why she was dumped. Perhaps because she was threatening— she threatened to grow up. She has no tail. The vet says she is a true, naturally born bobtail. Until you get used to her, it seems as if half a cat has just come into the room or out from under the couch.

I had threatened Karen's life if she didn't stop bringing us eating machines, and she pouted. So did Jill. Granddaughter Sarah swung into her awesome seven-year-old's let's-manipulate-granddad mode, and the terrible trio came on board. They are permanent, and surgery has been done. The good life lies ahead. They will never know hunger, neither will they know truculent weather unless they opt for it. They have it made! (When I die, if all that Hindu circular stuff is right, I want to come back as an animal in my house.)

One evening the awful three were playing in the hall near Teddy's H. BABB door when either Jill or I got the bright idea of seeing what Teddy's reaction would be to tiny kittens. He still had shown no signs of ever accepting anything with four legs except Emmy. And we had tested him—under tightly controlled conditions—from time to time. It would be nice to let H. BABB stand ajar. Teddy's room is one of the prettiest in the house, and it is a shame to have to slip in and out of it. Besides, it means an extra cat litter box, extra food and water dishes, just more things to remember not to forget.

On that fateful evening Jill and I carried the kittens into Teddy and Emmy's trysting place, ready to beat a quick retreat and save the kittens should our Jekyll-and-Hyde cat opt to play Mr. Hyde in response to our latest imposition.

But that is not how it went at all. Teddy came toward us with only the slightest hesitancy. In fact, he seemed to get giddier with every step he took. In minutes he was on his back with the mauling mites all over him. He pinned them one at a time and bathed them. Emmy did the strangest thing! Obviously miffed, she stalked out and hasn't been back to see Teddy since. Easy come, I guess, easy go. The kittens stayed.

Teddy mothered the kittens to an incredible degree. He is extraordinarily nurturing for a male, particularly a misanthrope-cat. The kittens insisted upon nursing, and Teddy accommodated by assuming the appropriate position. Amazingly, over the days, his nipples began to grow.

What all of this actually means, I don't know. An awful lot of genetic data have gotten twisted around one another and skewed out of shape. There have been misplaced responses to confusing signals, and the genders involved have become absolutely meaningless. Nothing, in fact, has dictated the scenario except Teddy's incredible tolerance on the one hand and total lack thereof on the other.

Bottom line, so to speak? Teddy found his true love in Emmy and then lost her within a few months. He now has three other companions who spend much of their time pouncing on his tail, which he obligingly swishes back and forth for them. They also nibble his whiskers and chew on his already well-scarred ears. He loves every minute of it. We have never seen him even a little cross with them, he of the ballistic trajectory at the sight of cat or dog.

What will happen when Mary, Martha, and Marmalade are old, too, I do not know. In all fairness, they cannot be assigned for life to mollycoddle Teddy's neuroses unless they elect to play that role. The strange foursome led by "mother" Teddy have emerged from solitary without becoming wacko over the other animals. They are now indoor-outdoor cats who hang out near Jill's orchid greenhouse. Teddy does not seek the company of other animals except the three "kids." And Emmy is very standoffish when she and Teddy encounter each other. Is there life after Emmy and M, M, and M? Stay tuned.

Teddy and the Gang, Plus One. Teddy (right foreground), Marmalade (behind him), and Martha Custis Washington (left) with an added attraction—Omari, very much in evidence (in the middle). The fact that Teddy now allows the likes of Omari to join his "family" is a sure sign of progress. This would have been an unthinkable scene even a few months ago. Like Teddy, Omari was a wild cat. Perhaps they have an understanding based on that common ground.

Alice Coming Home from a Walkabout. Where she goes, why she goes, what she does, nobody knows. She remains in excellent condition, and now that her sister is gone Alice has started discovering dogs. She has tried them out one at a time and particularly likes the Greyhounds and Topy the Whippet. On cool evenings she curls up with them and even lets them bathe her. She can be cranky and withdrawn one minute (perhaps planning her next safari) and quite pleasant and interactive the next. Whatever drummer Alice hears, he is distant indeed. Perhaps it is the drummer she seeks on her journeys.

4

Alice
and Elvira

ELVIRA HAS BEEN gathered; she has gone on ahead. But she and Alice started out together here at Thistle Hill, and initially the story of Alice has to include her sister, as well, for such they were when they walked the earth together in the secret pact that they shared with no one. They alone heard their music.

Their original owner, beautiful Marie Killilea, lived in Westchester, north of New York City. She was the author of several widely read books, the first of which, *Karen,* told the story of Marie's second daughter and their life of faith that saw them through terrible hardships. It was a story of courage and strength and was an extremely popular book in its day. For decades after it was published, Marie was still religiously answering letters by the score. Marie did everything religiously. That is what kept her alive for so long.

Marie had been literally dying for twelve years. She was tough and stubborn, but the combination of having only one lung and emphysema was wearing her down. It would win in the end. Marie became progressively allergic to just about everything, including Alice and Elvira. She called us one evening and told us that she couldn't be free to let go until her two beloved cats and her parrot had good homes. A phone call from Jill solved the parrot problem; it went to artist Ian Hornak on Long Island, and obviously we were the solution for the cats. Marie did finally let go after her little family was settled, and is now at peace.

Alice and Elvira were maiden ladies, littermates, rather small and elegant Seal-Point Siamese. They were so alike physically that I was never sure I could tell them apart. They didn't need or want the company of other animals, although they could co-exist in the same room, even at the other end of a couch, with another cat. They ignored dogs. Such untidy, noisy rowdies were beneath them, they seemed to indicate, but then, virtually everyone and everything was.

We never saw one of the ladies without the other.

Outside they walked side by side in regal splendor, scornful, it appeared, of the other animals who were always around, and inside they were *always* cuddled up together apart and aloof. That is not at all unusual for Siamese. They are typically snobs. We have had any number of Siamese, some of them among the dearest cats I have ever known, but I would hate to be judged socially by any of the lot. I am resigned to the fact that I could never measure up to their expectations, even if I were a lilac point, and lilac-point people are not that easy to find nowadays.

There was one distinction between Alice and Elvira that was very pronounced. Elvira was a love, a sweet and responsive cat with a sense of humor, and Alice was then as she is now, an awful crank! Almost everything in life was fine with Elvira, and nothing at all suited the scowling, loudly complaining Alice, the ultimate critic of all she beheld. For one the glass was half full, for the other half empty, and there was no middle position for either.

After they had done their mandatory imprinting time huddled together inside the house, Alice and Elvira were allowed, with the other cats, to come and go as they pleased. There are arguments that cats should not be allowed out at all, but that is virtually impossible at Thistle Hill Farm. We are an inside-outside family, and kids and adults and dogs and workers and delivery people are constantly coming and going. The house is a sieve. You would have to treat cats like footballs even to try to keep them from squirming past, shooting past, or otherwise getting out one door or another. And we do have space and are nowhere near a road. It is as close to a secure environment as we are likely to see except in that cats have a mild suicidal tendency no matter what the living conditions.

Sweet Elvira and cranky Alice eventually settled on an area for their operations that the other cats were underutilizing, although if there is a reason for that I don't know it. Perhaps it is just that at a place like Thistle Hill Farm, where at any one time there are many more niches than there are domestic creatures to occupy them, there are, at least temporarily, natural vacancies. That is inevitable, although they don't stay that way for long. Nature simply cannot tolerate vacuums. At the farm these areas are utilized by the Regulars as they are needed. Unfortunately, the smaller wildlife in these habitats have to yield. I wish that were not so, but nature has rules and one of them is that predators like cats eat prey and sometimes just kill for practice or perhaps, sadly, for recreation.

•

BULLETIN FROM THE BARN . . . Karen Dorn has come in and reported a new barn cat, a small, fuzzy gray job. Karen says it (no information as to its sex yet) is very shy, but it does seem settled in. As promised, we will report population changes including what happens with this new apparent addition. Heaven only knows the barn is big enough, and there is always enough food. . . .

•

I have watched lion, leopard, and cheetah make kills (hyena, too), and it isn't pretty. I have heard it suggested that prey animals switch off and don't feel all that pain and terror before they die. I would like to believe that, although in truth I don't know why nature would bother arranging for that since it would not offer a survival advantage, at least none that is apparent to me. I fear that nature . . . let's see if we can do this without a cliché, now . . . probably not. It's a jungle out there as much where two Siamese walk as where the lion or the leopard stalks.

The kennels is a rather large building, since it includes my four-room office suite (I am permanently, thereby, in the doghouse), and behind it is a communal dog run. This is about an acre enclosed by an electric fence that keeps even scent hounds at home. I am a firm believer in electric fences. Every time we have installed one I have tested it on my wrist, my elbow, and my shoulder. It is not a pleasant feeling but neither is it cruel. It is something animals really hate, startling. Every time a dog is put behind an electric fence for the first time you will hear a yelp within a few minutes. Rarely will you hear a second. Such fences are humane and in some cases essential.

Were it not for that fence some of the dogs would have to be chained or contained in individual runs, and we wouldn't like that any more than they would. Scent hounds are generally unreliable when it comes to staying on home turf. It they get a whiff of something enticing, they are gone. A Bloodhound would follow a skunk to Ohio on a whim and a whiff any day of the week. Hound people say a freely wandering Bloodhound is a dead dog.

Bloodhounds have no road sense at all. They see the world with their nose. This way, however, they have a full acre to cavort in with guillotine doors leading back into their indoor communal accommodations, which are commodious, clean, and warm.

WILLY (SWEET WILLIAM actually) is a very handsome Bloodhound. He is huge, a true giant, about 100 pounds. He has an enormous head and something like a pea for a brain. His ears are the size of prayer rugs. He is very, very dear, though, and we wouldn't dream of making fun of him, wrinkles and all. We make it seem

Sweet William (right), Followed by Rosebud, Sniffs Out Mysteries. Their run is huge (they now share it with Huxley the alpaca), but they still check it over thoroughly several times a day. Bloodhounds never lose faith in the possibility of discovering a great new smell, perhaps even an escaped convict. They are gentle giants with an incredible nose. We must drive them half crazy with the smells we create, some of which we can't even detect. They are behind an electric fence because they have no road sense and would be unable to resist a trail if they encountered one. If a deer or a fox or a skunk crossed our property during the night (and they often do) and the great hounds found the trail in the morning, goodbye, Bloodhounds!

as if we hang on his every yodel. He is all enthusiasm, about everything. He is enchanted with food above all else.

ROSE (actually, ROSEBUD) is a Bloodhound, too. She is lovely and dainty compared to Willy the moose. She has a whole marching band of her own drummers. She listens and gets in step when she hears what she wants to hear. She is sweet and beguiling, though, and full of the fun of life. Bloodhounds are engaging giants and I have heard that their slobber is quite good for the skin. I hope so.

A new kid on the block is Huxley, a young male alpaca. He shares the Bloodhound yard, separated from them by strands of "hot wire" until he is a little bigger. Blossom, a sheep, used to keep him company but she became ill. Maggie, the donkey, sometimes visits with Huxley now.

Approximately south of that "dog pasture" there is a rough pathway that runs through some pretty dense grass and bushes along the crest of a hill near the kitchen garden. The slope of that hill is steep and very thickly overgrown with brambles. As it is now, a human being could not negotiate it, not with hide intact. For a small, sinuous beast with a great sense of balance and the patience and sense to move slowly, it is apparently a piece of cake.

We often saw Elvira and Alice, the Asian ladies, as they came to be known, moving together along the path, always together, and sometimes over the edge and down the hillside, where they would quickly vanish. I envied them because that is where the original dump for this place was, well before the Civil War. I would love to get down there with my metal detector. I can't; the Asian ladies did. Wherever else you might encounter them, and that seemed to be a pretty random matter, sooner or later there they would be, picking their way through the rather unkempt area between the south end of the kennel yard and the crest of the hill and beyond. Very often you could locate them just by listening for Alice's complaining. She complained to bushes, birds, trees, me, and the clouds as well, I am sure.

The Odd Couple. Maggie, left, with her incredible ears and strange, curly coat, is the daughter of a wild-caught western burro, Pedro, who lives with our daughter's family. Humboldt, right is a chocolate-colored llama with a rather pleasant disposition for a cousin of the camel. Humboldt finds cats bemusing if not amusing. He will lean over a fence and watch them intently as they do their various "things."

The two devoted Siamese sisters went out every day the weather was good (if you really want to hear Alice complain you should hear her as she makes a U-turn at the door because she has found the weather outside untidy). By sundown, usually, they were back for some munching at the ad-lib bowl in the kitchen. One night they weren't. Jill and I, flashlights darting in all directions, *kitty-kitty-kittied* ourselves until we were blue in the face. Discouraged, we decided to go back to the house and wait for the two wanderers on the porch. They were there waiting for us when we arrived. They went inside without coaxing and headed for the food bowl as if nothing had changed. But it had.

It became a routine. They often stayed out late and sometimes overnight and that took some getting used to on our part. We tried the impossible, keeping them in, but it didn't work for so much as a day. They were determined to get out. They moved like ghosts at the speed of arrows, and they always did get out, singly or together. Until we finally conceded defeat, it seemed as if our lives consisted of running in circles calling to each other, "Check the closet in the bedroom," "Did you look downstairs, in the laundry?" "What about the dining room?" It is not possible to live that way, not with ten or twelve cats and as many dogs. Nose counting is fine to a point—it is a natural reflex among animal owners. But there has to be more to life than that.

One day an antique dealer friend of ours dropped off some things he had found for us. He was driving from a show in Atlanta, Georgia, to his home in West-hampton Beach, New York, and stopped to stay over with us. He made the ultimate although understandable mistake. He left the door of his truck ajar while he was loading up to go. He left for New York, and Elvira and Alice didn't come home that night. About eight hours into the next day the phone call came, right after he got around to unloading his van.

"Want to buy back two Siamese cats?" Grace Froehlich, a local animal rescue angel who was helping us out with the animals, offered to drive the five-hundred-mile round trip to retrieve Elvira and her malcontent sister, Alice. We now routinely ask all guests to check their cars before they leave. An open van half full of boxes and crates, even a car, is too much for any cat to resist. If the nosy little creatures hear the vehicle's owner approaching while they are exploring, what do they do? Hide! You can count on it.

Once Alice and Elvira were returned from their New York safari without prejudice, they resumed their joint careers on the farm where they had left off. They hung out in the same area, but usually in cover so thick we never found out what they did with most of their time. We assumed they hunted, but we never once saw them do it. If they weren't hunting back in that cover they must have completed one meticulous mapping survey, because back and forth they went day after day.

Sometimes the nights when they didn't come home turned into a week or more and we despaired for their survival. Again, we tried containment systems. There is just too much traffic here. Nothing we did worked. And eventually, after their walkabouts, the girls did always come home. They would be homebodies for a few days and on some days they didn't go out at all. Then the wanderlust would set in and off they would go until late in the evening, overnight, or for days. What summoned them? we asked; who or what called? Sometimes they overnighted within a couple of hundred feet of the house. It often seemed to depend entirely on the weather. Whenever we saw them they were together. They slept in each other's arms. Sweet and sour, they were like a pair of Siamese twins of another kind.

It went on like that with no real problems. It was just that Elvira and Alice insisted on doing their own scheduling. They were in lovely condition, their coats glistened. Little wonder, they groomed each other incessantly and seemed happy and well adjusted. Well, at least Elvira did. Alice? Well, after all, she was Alice. Beyond that nothing need be said.

Then, one morning, the thing all animal owners dread happened. When we got up, Alice was alone waiting to come in. The two of them had been gone two nights, as I recall, and now cheerful, upbeat Elvira was missing. Alice sat on the kitchen windowsill looking out. She must have known what happened, but it was forever contained within her.

We looked, of course, day after day, and we called until we were hoarse, in the woods, around the barn, along the girls' secret path south of the dog pasture, everywhere we could think to go. We had a string of puzzled cats following wherever we went. We were, after all, making all kinds of *Here, kitty* sounds. We put treats out as bait, but the other cats ate them. Why wouldn't they? There was no sign of Elvira. Not a clue.

Slowly, what had been reality all along was accepted. Mischance had befallen sweet Elvira. It could have been any number of things, if one is willing to deal with possibilities and not just probabilities. She could have been stolen, perhaps even accidentally. She could have climbed into a delivery truck. Two or three a day stop here—UPS, FedEx, U.S. Mail, and others, too. But, alone? It didn't seem likely. We canvassed the regular drivers. It hadn't been their trucks.

Did curiosity get Elvira? Or did the two girls go all the way out to the road? A car, a truck? Was it more natural than that—a fox, an owl, a wandering dog? Could she have encountered a copperhead or a rattlesnake and gone off into a brambly area to die alone, but in peace?

We'll never know the answer, and that is the really miserable part. She was very friendly and as pretty as her kind can be, so perhaps she was stolen and is safe and comfortable although with some strange vestigial memory of the farm. Although we miss good-natured, gentle Elvira, we can't be missing her as much as we think Alice is missing her in her own secret way.

Alice is alone now. She still won't take up with the other cats. Perhaps she will try with Teddy, since his infants are now tough little kids. After all, he is royalty, too, and she might even approve, unless he becomes ballistic at the sight of her approaching "his" greenhouse. *(He did!)*

Alice still complains a lot. We often see her alone up on the old stomping grounds she used with her sister. Is there something special there that attracted them then and attracts Alice now? Can Alice possibly be looking for Elvira? Do existentialists—and cats are nothing if they are not that—have memories? They can't look ahead, but can they look back? (It is interesting. A short paragraph about people, okapi, or wombats would be unusual if it contained four question marks. Somehow, when you write about cats, they seem perfectly natural.)

Alice spends more time near the house now and only goes out for an hour or so at a time. She is still punishing in her attitude, but she is needy, and we try to fill in. Sometimes she will sit in your lap, but not for long. She inevitably has something rude to mew as she gets down.

Life goes on here at Thistle Hill Farm. The cats as it is with all of the other creatures get swept along. Perhaps without tolerant Elvira to hear her out, Alice will settle down and find things more to her liking. We'll see, but Alice seems on a safer schedule now that she is alone. Perhaps Elvira was the more adventuresome of the two.

P.S. Alice has made an important decision. She obviously doesn't like being alone after all but will not take up with another cat. She has picked out a dog instead! It is Lilly, our soft and extremely gentle Greyhound who mothers everything. Yesterday we saw Alice rub against the sleeping Lilly with a faraway look in her eyes. This morning the recumbent Lilly had Alice between her forelegs and was bathing her. Alice twisted to get more, more, more. Who would have thought it? She always seemed so disdainful of dogs. All the time she was a closet dog lover. Two days later: *Alice has now taken up with Mr. Sweet-Face himself, the Whippet Topaz. She has seen the light. She has found the truth that awaits all cats who will only dare seek it. (See Chapter 9.)*

Himself! Steakums in all his glory. When he was res-cued from a traveling petting zoo in Virginia, he had been locked in a truck for four days without food or water. The humane rescue people assured us he was a "miniature steer" and would not get any larger than a large dog. He is now approaching 1,200 pounds. Some dog! Still, he is a cheerful, peaceful resident and ignores cats and all dogs except Duncan, whom he would like to massacre.

5

The Farm Schedule

FREE SPIRITS though they might be, and they surely are that insofar as it is possible, the cats of Thistle Hill Farm still have to match their individual lifestyles to a series of grander schemes. They do not exist in a vacuum.

First, there is the weather, which is the single most influential force for all of us. There are the other animals of the several species that live here, and there are the human beings and the feeding schedules we the people are willing to establish. There are schedules inside and outside the house, the barn, and the kennels. We do not like chaos any better than cats do. Whether or not to bend is all part of that ring of positive and negative incentives. Ultimately the cats do. They have to. It isn't so much that they must surrender as simply accommodate our needs, which ultimately suit their needs.

If we are having a buffet dinner party, and there are platters of ham and turkey, the cats have to be banished outside if the weather is good or restricted to a locked room if it isn't. We try to do what is best for them. If they have to see their veterinarian, for example, it won't be when they feel like going, or they would never go. It has to be when the veterinarian and someone here, probably Karen, have agreed on an appointment. The cat is not consulted, it is transported. We have to believe that we are better at considering their well-being with perspective than they are.

It is a perfectly reasonable assumption, the kind every parent has dared make as well as every pet owner. In that sense the blithe spirit free to the sky and the wind is a lovely concept that can only be partially realized.

The human cast in the ongoing Thistle Hill Farm drama shrinks and swells like a pulse beat. Jill and I live here and so does Jill's mother, Phyllis Barclay. An English lady (Henley-on-Thames) of decidedly literary bent and generous elocution, she is, at ninety, what I believe is frequently called remarkable. She cooks when she feels like it, gardens, travels to New York and Florida alone.

She feeds animals, makes toys for her great-grandchildren, is a professional storyteller, and has both a keen mind and a better memory than I have. Of course, there are genes. Her mother lived to ninety-eight, her aunt to one hundred and two. Her baby sister is now eighty-eight.

Karen Dorn is here four days a week as farm manager and general factotum. She orders animal food, works with the animals, paints, helps clean, coordinates with the veterinarians and the farrier, mows, and does about a dozen other chores. Jill says she is going to kill herself if Karen ever leaves. Seems a little extreme to me, but then, Jill is nothing if not extreme.

Tacker is Karen's husband. (How can anyone call another human being Ferdinand, for heaven's sake! What were his parents thinking?) Tacker is a licensed electrician, he is a pretty darn good joiner, and he has a work ethic matched only by that of his wife. He is here part-time. When he starts with his list—*"Add four electrical outlets in the kitchen, move the thermostat in the dining room, move the outlet from baseboard height to table level behind the flower-shaped end table in the dining room, repair the broken leg on the antique rocking horse, replace the doorknobs and latch in the peach guest room, and put a new pane of glass in the window in the bathroom at the top of the stairs"*—it is whirlwind time. He will literally come to us for new lists in about an hour and a half. It took a little longer to redo my bathroom completely with the new plumbing, floor, ceiling and all, to add a thirty-by-twelve-foot screened front porch, lay a new brick pathway down from the drive, and design and build the new pool house. If he leaves, I am going to kill myself. That is not extreme. It would, in fact, be a relatively mild reaction to the end of the world.

Pam Holder is our animal lady, and she feeds weekends and every afternoon and on those mornings when Karen won't be here. She is fantastic with all of the animals; she has a magic touch. When her pickup turns into the drive Steakums shakes the earth with gigantic, rolling moos, Maggie brays with enormous enthusiasm, and the hounds bay their musical best. The horses, along with Humboldt and Maggie, run up to the fence. (No, Maggie doesn't bray and run at the same time. I think perhaps she can't. I don't know about chewing gum.) Steakums gets pushy and Fat Susan Jane, our cow, waddles behind and blinks.

Nancy Thurm and Carol Asten are cleaning ladies. Neither of them will clean a floor with a mop. By their standards a mop is a symbol of decadence, of a failed society. A floor for them is done on one's hands and knees with a small brush. I think they would use a toothbrush if we let them. Other people help from time to time depending on what is happening. Doug Leister is an incredibly skilled carpenter. All that coming and going, not to mention going and coming, underscores why cat confinement short of a cattery with cages just can't work, not here.

There is another full family as well. In fact, there are two. Daughter Pamela, a successful publishing executive, and her husband, Joe Rupert, a highly skilled printing executive, and their two daughters, Sarah and Hannah, live fifteen minutes away. They are often here. During pony camp season, since the camp by good luck is on the Gentry farm, Weathered Wood, just across the way, Sarah lives here five days a week.

The Rupert clan does not come to visit with any of their cats, who would be strangers on the ground and could get confused and stray. They do, however, often come with a dog, or two, or three, just to add diversity to the biomass. Chloë, the most frequent visitor, is random bred, has three legs, and is one of the cutest, happiest dogs I have ever known. It is sad that so many people give up on "handicapped" pets. Chloë can't count. She can't understand a concept like birth defect and doesn't realize that she should have a leg in the right front corner, too, so she runs with the pack. She is such a joyous little creature that the dogs here, her "cousins," are always delighted to see her. Everybody wags their tails and everybody sniffs everybody. It is just a pleasant time, genuinely so. The cats seek high ground, and Alice laments loudly. Chloë's exuberance is too much for the likes of them.

Zack, one of the best-natured dogs in the world, a senior citizen, a massive yellow Lab, came over until recently, when he lost out to cancer, and enjoyed a good old-fashioned sniff-up with the best of them. Annie, a two-thousand-year-old JRT (Jack Russell Terrier) tags along occasionally and engages in her favorite game, recreational barking.

Son Clay, a forensic psychiatrist and naval officer,

his wife, Sheila, and their two children, Joshua and Ab-aigeal, as previously indicated, live in Connecticut, but they are often down. Joshua has lived here with his cousin Sarah during pony camp season and now Abaigeal has started as well. Both couples will eventually build houses of their own on the farm, and we will have the best of all possible worlds—privacy and instant reunion. We love the gathering of the clan. The animal population and all of the other farm amenities will only increase. There are already four generations (of people) in the mix. It will be interesting to see if we can make it five.

When we have guests, and we very often do (since we do live out in the boonies, guests are more often overnighters than just eat-and-run types), and staff are around, and the family is gathered, we need revolving doors. The place fairly hums with people and animals. It is amazing to see *and* hear.

When Karen or Pam arrives, usually at seven o'clock or shortly thereafter, the kennel's two guillotine doors are opened and the food prepared for the Blood-hounds. Diets are carefully monitored and only premium foods are used, because hounds, especially Bloodhounds, are subject to a lethal condition known as "bloat" in which gas gets trapped in the stomach and they go into shock. It is a frequent killer of these handsome but highly specialized dogs. Medicating (things like routine worming) is done at this time and notes made of interest and importance to whoever will be seeing the dogs next. Cat food is then prepared. Karen enters the data into

Maggie, Humboldt, and Sherry in One of the Front Pastures. One is as sweet as the other, and even the toddler grandchildren can move freely among them. Unchallenged by life, they are never challenging. Peace and benevolence are contagious. Most animals will adopt it as a lifestyle quite willingly.

her computer. The kennel is cleaned, the kennel kitchen tidied. The girls have very high standards. The kennel kitchen is immaculate. No odor is allowed. There is a great deal of interacting with the dogs. If I am home and working in the office next door I visit with the three kennel dogs again by mid-morning.

The cat food, both moist and dry, is carried across the way to the upper or loft level of the barn. The real barn cats are fed along with any of the other Regulars who have decided on a little rustic R&R and have spent their night in the barn.

Next comes the hoofed stock. We keep all of our stock together, except Huxley the Alpaca, and that is a temporary arrangement. The four horses, one donkey, two head of cattle, and one llama are a unit; and their barn is an ad-lib option on the lower or stable level. The main aisle and several stalls are always left open and the animals can come in or stay out in the paddock area plus two large pastures, whatever pleases them. Only in freezing rain, and not always then, do they usually decide to get under cover. We are soon going to add to their options with a couple of pole barns. In the winter they all look like yaks and can turn their rumps toward almost any weather system and wait it out. It can never get cold enough or hot enough to worry a llama. This is, after all, Maryland and not a plateau in the Andes.

Pam or Karen checks the water (in one-hundred-gallon troughs) and drains and replaces it if the animals have been messy, puts out hay for communal eating, and supplies feed individually in open stalls. Soon everybody is munching and peace reigns on a population of contented beasts.

•

BULLETIN . . . This just in from Pamela. The new barn cat has been seen again. It is apparently not well groomed, obviously very young, and extremely shy. It was seen at a flat-out run. That's all we know, except it seems to be hanging out here, and with the regular morning food offerings and the shelter potential in a hayloft, it will probably stay. For a small cat, though, and apparently this is quite a young kitten, it can be a hazardous world. We will soon have to think about trapping it for some essential motivational adjustments.

•

At the house, by eight o'clock, the dogs have been let out. Topy, the Whippet, and his Greyhound friends are probably doing laps on the hill in front of the house. Lilah, the Pug, is snorting and goose-stepping around out front, making sure the world knows it is in luck because she has survived another night. Sam, the Yorkshire Terrier, is yapping, too.

The cats are let out if they want to go. Some come in from their night on the porch or in the barn. It is a time of shifting and straightening personal agendas. The cats' food is ad lib, so they don't have to be fed on schedule. Their communal bowls are checked throughout the day and at bedtime. The three stainless-steel buckets that serve as watering holes for all of the house animals are checked and refreshed or emptied and washed and then refilled. Duncan, the Border Collie, is let out and begins his daylong job of running the whole farm. DUNCAN, whose late father, Mike, co-starred in

Duncan Between Chores. Possessed by his genes, Duncan the Border Collie works from dawn till late at night. He is absolutely certain that nothing will work on the farm unless he is at the core, pushing, shoving, guiding, advising. His father was Mike the Wonder Dog, who starred in Down and Out in Beverly Hills. *Duncan was a gift from Clint Rowe, who owned and trained Mike for his film and television appearances.*

the film *Down and Out in Beverly Hills,* always has places to go and things to do. He is the busiest dog I have ever known. When the other dogs don't feel like being herded and the horses threaten to kick him over the barn, he plays soccer by himself. At night he is exhausted. Humboldt the llama would like to stomp him into the mud and often tries to. Maggie the donkey puts her ears back and chases him flat out around the pasture. Still, he has his work to do, dangerous or not. His genes tell him so.

The dogs are soon winded and are back asking for their one meal a day. The two macaws have their food and water dishes removed and cleaned and replenished at the same time, and their cages are cleaned. Some of the house cats will have gone up to the barn by now to share a little of the rations put out there. It isn't long before everyone is content. If the weather is bad the cats may opt for the house or the barn. If it is a nice day, they typically head out to their respective morning turfs to do their own thing.

That is the basic schedule. It seldom varies, and if it does we hear about it. If the stock is fed a little behind schedule morning or evening—the water, hay, and feed routine is done twice a day—Maggie brays the leaves off the trees; Steakums moos pathetically; the horses nicker, whinny, snort, and stomp; the dogs bark and yowl; Humboldt hums; and down in the kitchen, if the cat dish runs dry the cats meow in disgust, particularly Alice, who goes cross-eyed with rage. It is better for all concerned if things stay pretty much on schedule. It is easier than trying to explain human failings to all these other species. Oh yes, the macaws. If their dishes are not filled with fresh fruit appropriately sliced and diced when they go to them, they blister the paint with their intolerant *crawks* and *squawks*. They brook no nonsense. They also know about a dozen words each—in English —some of which are not polite. To a macaw, life is a four-letter word.

Why do we do it, at this order of magnitude? Why thirty or more pets? Because they are alive, and that is

what living is all about. If animals didn't get into trouble as often as they do we would probably have fewer of them. Certainly every cat here now except one was given sanctuary. If you are not going to sustain life, what right do you or I have to own land. Land, even small parcels like this, is the breast on which living things, plant and animal, wild and domestic, nurse. That is what Thistle Hill Farm and our lives are all about. And the cats know it.

Outside the Kennel Door, a Feeding Station. Jean Valjean (left), Omari, barely visible (center), and Xnard (pronounced Snard) wait at one of several stations where cat food is put out twice every day. Strangers passing through dine at these stations as well. The dismantled shipping-crate halves make dining in the rain a little more pleasant and help keep dogs out of the cats' dinner.

A Jungle of Legs. Horses and donkeys and the like must seem obscene in size to a cat. But I find that once they get over the initial shock, most cats ignore the monsters. Martha Custis Washington takes the sun without regard for even Sheba, fuzzy in the left background, who is a Belgian draft horse. She is confident that none of the giants will step on her, and she is justified in her faith. Hoofed animals are comfortable around cats, and I have never heard of a cat getting into trouble that way.

94

6

The Crew
in the Barn

THE PEOPLE who lived at Thistle Hill Farm before it was known by that name clearly did not care for animals the way we do—for or about them. As a matter of fact, their tenure was a classic story of pathological indifference and neglect. When we first arrived (we had not moved down from New York, yet) there were a Thoroughbred mare and her yearling son running pretty much wild and unattended. Gates were open, and they ran from pasture to pasture. The house was unoccupied, and it was really kind of spooky, just the animals being here, no people. Somehow they seemed lonely, but that is probably projection. It was, though, like an opening scene to a murder movie.

The young stallion had tangled with some barbed wire, and one eyelid was hanging down in ribbons over his eye. The lacerations seemed to be infected although the yearling was so wild you couldn't get near him. My daughter was the first to notice this intolerable condition and called the owner. He thanked her, without conveying very much conviction. In fact, he sounded downright bored, but he did promise to call a vet. Two weeks later nothing had been done. That, apparently, was typical. With further prodding by my tenacious daughter (when it comes to animals, you really don't want Pamela prodding you), the man did finally arrange for a vet to come, but all there was left to do was cosmetic surgery. The young stallion, although woefully neglected, had weathered the storm.

There was a Smooth Collie living in the barn when we first visited the farm. Neighbors told us that she had not been spayed. She had had litter after litter of offspring over a period of nine years although no one knew how many puppies had been born in total. Worse, no one could account for the fate of so much as a single puppy! They were born in a corner of the loft, she nursed them, and then they just vanished one by one. It is possible somebody came by and took one, but no one can really attest to the survival of any of them. I have never seen another Smooth Collie in this area that could possibly count as even a single survivor. Of course, her mates had to have been random, and the puppies more than likely would not look like her at all.

The dog had never been allowed in the house but lived as a wild thing in the barn loft that has a ground-level entrance from the driveway. It seems unbelievable that had gone on for so long. She was completely unattended and probably had a litter after every heat, as many as seventeen or eighteen litters, probably averaging out to five puppies each—as many as ninety puppies without a known survivor. Her former owner later admitted that she had never even been given a name, but was simply referred to as "the dog." Since there were three children in the family, it is difficult to believe that she wasn't named. Our children in their day and our four grandchildren today pin a name on everything that moves or breathes and not just a few things that do neither. When we were looking the farm over, Pamela named her Fantine (all of the members of the barn crew, except one, were named for characters in *Les Misérables*). Fantine went home with Pamela and Joe and saw the inside of a house probably for the first time. She was, surprisingly, affectionate and fine with the children. Of course, she was fine with cats. She had spent her whole life with them in the loft. She lived on as an orthodox, card-carrying couch potato for two more years with constant veterinary care for a variety of skin ailments. While she was living the good life she hated to go out of the house for even a couple of minutes. She had discovered what soft meant, and she was hanging on to it. She craved attention—all this as if she were trying desperately to make up for all that lost time.

It is no mystery how Fantine had survived. The people from whom I bought the farm had simply moved away making no provision for their animals at all. They had rarely fed Fantine when they lived here. It is no surprise that they didn't come back and see to her well-being after they had come apart as a family and moved away. Her survival was the result of the big hearts of Ditty Gentry and her daughter Galvin across the way. Every day, no matter what the weather, Ditty and Galvin, both of whom felt less than kindly toward the former owner, brought the cat and dog food to the barn and saw to it that at least one basic need of the abandoned animals was covered. The horses had enough forage available to them as well as a stream (where the barbed wire was strung) to make it. They weren't in great shape, but they weren't starving either.

The story of Fantine and the cats and what was and was not done for them is an example of the best and the worst in our species. Are there people who can get into a car and simply drive off, leaving their animals without any provisions? Yes, there are. Are there people who will spend their own time and money trying to compensate for the evil behavior of other people, people they don't even like? Yes again, there are. When I later questioned the former owner about the cats and the dog, he brushed it off with a patent lie about having made arrangements with someone to come and see to their needs every day. Someone came, all right, but he didn't even know about it, nor, we can surmise, did he care. So much for him.

And the cats! We think there were four the first time we came here, but if so, one vanished before we moved in. When we were finally on the grounds for good, there were three. There was a small, essentially white cat with tabby splotches (she would become Cosette); a female very much like her, her daughter (who never got a name); and an all-black tom later to be known as Jean Valjean. As had been the case with Fantine, breeding had been random and uncontrolled. Cats breed at an early age, seven months, at least that early, and do not worry about our sophisticated concepts, things like incest. Nature doesn't like inbreeding, but individual animals can't worry about it. They just respond to biological signals opportunistically.

It appears obvious that Cosette and company are seriously inbred. In form, not color, they are rather like little North African wildcats. That would happen if inbreeding went on for enough generations—father to daughter, mother to son, and back and forth among littermates. Cosette and kin are close-coupled or cobby (not long and sinewy); they have short legs; they crouch low when they move; and they have short, fat faces. They have a wildcat feeling about them, a "look." One can imagine them along the banks of the Nile and at oases in the Sahara.

As with Fantine, no one knows how many litters were born to that little cat population in the barn, or who bred with whom, for the mothers of the litters were often little more than kittens themselves. There must have been literally hundreds of kittens. It will not come as a surprise that no one knows what became of those bushel baskets full of kittens. If you take two cats—an unspayed queen and an unaltered male—the *potential,* if all of their kittens lived, in just seven years, would be 150,000 kittens. It doesn't work out that way because there is so much mischance for cats, but only an awful lot of unnecessary dying keeps those staggering figures from coming true.

Kittens by the score had died up there at the barn, obviously, but all we had to deal with was three, then two, and now, while this book is under way, one—plus, of course, the new little gray job I have never seen personally, but about which we are getting bulletins.

Cosette's unnamed daughter died before we had trapped any of the barn cats for surgery and shots. I recall her as being even wilder, even more terrified of us than her mother or her brother were. Then, one morning, there she was, like a hanged corpse on a lamppost on London Bridge. It took a very long ladder to retrieve her hard, cold body.

There are characteristics that distinguish a bank barn such as the one we have here on the farm from other barns. It is built on two levels, into the side of a hill, and typically will have entrances on opposite sides, one upstairs, the loft, and one down, the stable. The foundation is fieldstone and the woods used throughout are hard. As mentioned elsewhere the big barn here

—and it is very big—is oak and chestnut. Another characteristic is the spacing of the vertical planks of wood in the loft part. There are gaps from half an inch to an inch and a half between the planks to allow maximum air circulation around the hay. That prevents heat from building up and causing so-called self-ignition or spontaneous combustion. Our barn, built before 1850, has very old planking, obviously, and some areas that are showing their age. Pieces of planking have pulled away from the cross members and curled; some have splintered; some of the air-circulation gaps are now very uneven. The whole barn is scheduled to be restored in the next few years, it is on the list, but in the meantime it is a kind of spectacular icon of rural America as it once was when the work ethic didn't have a name. It didn't need one.

Cosette's daughter—then, I would guess, about six months old—had either been walking along a cross beam or jumping from one to another inside the barn, so very high up that it really is a second loft level. Perhaps she was swatting at pigeons, starlings, or sparrows. Somehow the poor little thing had gotten her head and all of her right front leg including her right shoulder out through a Y-shaped gap between planks. At that point she had apparently lost her footing inside, slid down the slope of the Y into the crotch of the opening. There she was, the rest of her body dangling on the inside of the barn, her head and foreleg jutting out on the outside. She had obviously strangled. Cats, Lord love 'em, get into such incredible trouble. I had

The Death Trap. Jean Valjean's unnamed sister died in this Y-slot in the old oak planking before we even got to know her. Somehow she got her head and one foreleg through, lost her footing inside, and slid down, strangling herself. It was a sad introduction to Thistle Hill Farm. The world is a dangerous place for cats without human contact, although this kind of accident could happen to any cat.

never gotten to know this cat, kitten really, but her dying so painfully was sad. Jill cried. I just felt a big lump. For all the comfort the world had offered her in so short a life, it can be said, and I believe this is literally so, she should never have been born. She was a cruel mistake. I blame my predecessors here for what happened. Senseless life, when the brutality of misadventure is all that lies ahead, is so easy to prevent. There is no mystery to it, just simple human compassion.

My son, Clay, as noted, is a forensic psychiatrist. He explained the kind of behavior we saw here to me on a recent visit. There are people who simply do not have the ability to care, to feel for anybody or anything else. They cannot exhibit concern that is remotely akin to pity. It is as if they were missing an essential piece of their anatomy. They are, really, lacking in their emotional anatomy. If you have no eyes you cannot see, if you have no ears you cannot hear, if you are missing this unnamed part of your mind you cannot feel for anything, except your own instant gratification and fulfillment. Therein are the rapists of the world and many other violent types.

Infants do not have the power of concern, but they develop it in an appropriate social, familial environment. Some relatively few infants do not. It is a pitiful yet somehow horrifying case of arrested development. Perhaps, like Cosette's daughter, they are victims, too, and should never be born. They are the world's hurters and harmers. If they do not overtly do evil themselves, they tolerate it. Not doing anything to stop pain, fear, and suffering in other creatures, human or otherwise, is little different from inflicting these ultimate ills yourself.

This chapter was to be about Cosette, mother of that ill-starred kitten, and about her son, but now we have lost Cosette, too. Let me carry her story along to her death.

After the kitten had died (we had really just moved in), we set large box traps baited with lovely tuna fish that got higher and higher as the hours without refrigeration passed. We soon had both cats and with little thanks from them we transported them to the hospital.

They were, in fact, in a yowling rage, nearly mad with fear over their first experience with confinement by the time they were handed over to the vet-tech.

He was neutered, she was spayed, and they both got shots for everything from leukemia to panleukopenia to rabies. They were not happy campers. In a few days they were released back into the barn. Except for their sulking and injured pride and the telltale bald patch on Cosette's abdomen, you would never know that such terrible things had been done to them. In fact, they experienced no aftereffects. Cats and dogs seldom do.

Veterinarians today perform these procedures, castration and ovario-hysterectomies, so many times I think most of them could manage either job just about blindfolded. I don't think most lay people really appreciate the skill and versatility of today's veterinarian. Backed by laboratories and board-certified specialists available for referral or consultation, a clinician today routinely deals with surgical and medical problems that would have been all but unthinkable as manageable crises even thirty years ago. When it is elective and not an acute or critical matter, the level of skill available and the ease and speed with which that skill is delivered is nothing if not awesome.

And so Cosette and Jean Valjean settled back into their new life unable to reproduce, with no urge to wander and fight other cats. They were fortified, we thought, against all diseases they were likely to encounter in any transient cat population that came our way. Cat diseases are typically highly contagious.

Rabies, against which our animals including our cats are protected, is a matter of grave concern all along the East Coast of the United States. Contrary to what most people believe, it is as common, in some places even more common, among cats as among dogs.

About forty years ago there was a serious outbreak of rabies among raccoons in the northern counties of Florida. It was soon clear that it was a full-blown epizootic (the equivalent among animals of an epidemic among people) and the principal reservoir (rabies almost inevitably has a single reservoir species in an epizootic) was the raccoon. In very short order there wasn't a single county anywhere in Florida or Georgia that was not reporting rabid raccoons, and it was already moving into other species both wild and domestic.

The scenario was repeated in South Carolina, but, what was first thought to be mysteriously, it skipped North Carolina and appeared in Virginia. Cats and dogs were dying or being killed when they became suspect. The disease in man or beast is one hundred per cent fatal unless caught before it has had time to incubate and is headed off with postexposure prophylaxis, shots.

The North Carolina mystery was soon cleared up. Before it had time to invade the Tarheel State, hunters from Virginia had trapped some raccoons in South Carolina and released them back home to run and tree with their dogs. Naturally, some of the relocated animals were infected, and the inevitable happened. In short order the infection reached North Carolina naturally, and it moved very quickly since it was moving north from South Carolina and south from artificially infected Virginia at the same time.

Maryland was next, and with no idea that I would ever live here, not even a remote hint, I was down here not far from Thistle Hill Farm with my television crew doing a news report on the epizootic's invasion of the north. Pennsylvania was hit, with both cows and horses being infected not far north of here. New Jersey got it next and now it is in New York and moving across Connecticut. While all of this has been going on, a second epizootic with the red fox as its principal reservoir has been moving south from Canada.

Anyone with animals has to be concerned, especially on a farm where species like cats and dogs are likely to inspect any animals that come onto their turf. Not protecting pets against rabies is unthinkable, but before we got here the single dog and unknown numbers of cats went unprotected. How many of the puppies and kittens that were born in the hay loft of our barn may have died of that dread disease is anyone's guess, and that is all it can ever be. The little animals were vanishing regularly while the disease was moving through this area like the plague.

A serum to protect a person or an animal against an infectious disease is a piece of extremely complex chemical machinery, and like any other man-made device, it can go wrong. A fault in manufacture or packaging, a problem in transport or storage, any number of things can seriously reduce or even erase a serum's viability. Perfection is seldom attainable, unfortunately.

One of the diseases cat owners have traditionally dreaded most is feline leukemia. It is ferociously infectious and insidious in its spread through a cat population. Years ago, before there was a serum for leukemia in cats, we had a large cat population. There were thirteen animals including several of the nicest cats I have ever known. We were asked to give a home to a waif of a kitten and she was "hot." The kitten died, taking eight of our thirteen cats with her. It was like a scene created by Dante. One after another they became ill. One after another they died. Why the remaining five cats with the same exposure didn't become ill is a mystery, but, then, so is this virus-driven disease. I have known many "cat people" who feel that ten cats is the maximum number there should be in a population to keep risk down. When we reached fourteen with the addition of that little kitten we were all but swept away by a wave of death. It really was awful, and some very old friends were carried off. It seems now they were the walking dead.

Naturally, our cats at Thistle Hill Farm are given feline leukemia shots along with rabies and all of the others. If we forget when it is booster time there is a computer at our small animal veterinarian's office that remembers. Karen's computer does, too. Apparently, the last batch of serum used on our cats was imperfect. Out of ten cats here at the farm, three died of leukemia in quick succession, from a disease against which they had been given a protective shot. Why the other seven were not infected is again a mystery. Even though there is now statistically very good protection, the disease is still both mysterious and insidious.

Among the three who died was poor little Cosette. Actually, we didn't wait for her to die. She was so sick when we found her that she could no longer sit up, she could barely move. She didn't resist when Karen picked her up. She just went limp. She went to the hospital, and the veterinarian just shook his head. Her time of pain was quickly over. Heaven help us, Siafu, perhaps the very nicest single cat I have ever known, and Fluffy Louise were the other two. They will remain a part of our account here, as will Cosette, until they drop off along the way.

While she was alive Cosette did not hang out with her son the way Alice and Elvira stayed together. They were often in the same area, usually where food was being offered or near shelter when the weather was dicey, but they were not limpets glued together as the Siamese ladies were. The focus of both of their lives, though, was the barn. For Jean Valjean it still is.

Both of the barn cats quickly adapted to the cats that came south from New York. The dogs, too, offered no problem. They are not aggressive toward cats, so there really never was a reason for them to be defensive except as something like a pro-forma ritual. Typically on the hill between here and the barn there would be Cosette and Jean Valjean, four or five of the house cats, and any number of dogs, sunning themselves, doing laps, with Omari marching through their midst looking like Groucho Marx with yet another stick offering. No problem at all. It is all just an exercise in tolerance: *"You're O.K., I'm O.K., we're O.K."*

Cats make a wonderful audience. They are great watchers and whether or not what they see is amusing, bemusing, or something else to them, I cannot say. Yesterday, there were six deer in a secret area of the marsh where they hang out. It is an area that can't be seen except from a certain two windows in the house. We keep binoculars near one of the windows and yesterday, while I watched the deer, I saw three cats watching them, too, from a spot very much closer to them. Jean Valjean and Omari were in the audience along with a cat I do not know. It will be interesting to see if that black-and-white cat shows up again. (He has!)

What would interest cats watching deer browse enough to attract three of them? They certainly have seen deer before. Today I saw Jean Valjean watching a fat pheasant hen feed in the same deer yard. It is as if he goes on safari to watch wildlife. Jill and I have been on twenty-six African safaris over the years where we watched wild animals feed, mate, kill, care for their young, just do their thing. It is endlessly fascinating. We have watched animals in the Arctic, in the Amazon basin, in the Andes, and a number of times in the Galapagos Islands, too. Was what we were doing all that different from what the cats do here?

When new animals come to us, the cats all show

Steakums and Fat Susan Jane Make a Smooth Tennis Net Crossing. Duncan heads the other way to make certain the pasture has been cleared, since he can't count noses. At first, Steakums wanted to make a shish kebab of the pushy Border Collie, but they have reached an accommodation of sorts. It can be dicey at times, though.

marked interest, at least most do, with Jean Valjean among them. Remember, with the recent death of his mother he is the longest-term resident here although nowhere near the oldest animal. Maggie the donkey with her outrageous voice kept Jean Valjean and Cosette fascinated for several days. Of course they had the apartment above hers because our hoofed stock is locked in a stall with the upper door open for at least their first week. That allows the horses, especially, to come over and visit and get used to the stranger's smell before they are in a position to do any kicking or biting. Humboldt the llama elicited the same fascinated response. Like farm cats everywhere the cats here, the barn lot and the house gang both, are perfectly comfortable around

livestock. They walk very close to creatures that may weigh three to four hundred times as much as they do with complete confidence. Livestock appear to be comfortable around cats, too. I am convinced, in fact, that the larger animals like the smaller ones because they are familiar and not at all threatening. Cats, very often including Jean Valjean, sit near and watch the larger domestic animals when they are not on safari spying on wildlife. I wonder what they see that they haven't seen before.

As for what there is to watch:

STEAKUMS is an almost totally Hereford steer. What the odd other influence might be will remain forever a mystery. Steakums came to us as a rescue case from an abandoned traveling petting zoo. He and a host of other animals had been locked in a tractor trailer beside a highway in Virginia for four days without food or water. When the police broke in, it was 104°F. inside. Steakums has a rusty red tear painted by his genes on one white cheek, just below his eye. When the sun is high but the air is cool, he thinks he is a bull. We dissuade him. It is easier than climbing fences. He weighs well over a half a ton, but he is a dear. We would let him live out his macho fantasy, but there are the grandchildren to consider. He seems to understand. A little "pretend" is okay, but no goring or maiming. It is enough in life to look tough. Acting tough is not necessary.

FAT SUSAN JANE is the older woman in Steakums's life. She enjoys the company of younger men. She is twenty-two or -three now, the oldest cow our vet has ever seen. No one else, it seems, lets them grow old. Here at Thistle Hill Farm she can grow as old as she wants. She was all black once. Now her face is almost all gray. She is a little stiff at times, but stubborn. She takes aspirin the size of a bricklayer's thumb to help her through the damp weather. She is truly devoted to Steakums and licks him all over when he lies out in the sun. They are a nice couple, quiet, orderly; they never quarrel and are clearly as suited to each other as they can be. They have a Far Side quality to them. Gary Larson would approve.

MAGGIE is, I am sure, the donkey with the longest

ears in the world. They look as though they should have an electronic component. Her soulful song of greeting, delivered with her head held high and her nostrils flaring, makes the hills and the valleys hereabouts ring. It is right out of the Grand Canyon. Ferde Grofé would approve. It is a musical event that sounds far more like a movie sound effect than something an animal should be able to do. Maggie has amazing curly hair and the daintiest feet you ever saw. She is closely bonded to a tall, dark, handsome, and aloof stranger from a distant land. Together they follow you like dogs when you enter the pasture.

SHEBA is a Belgian draft horse with the biggest butt I have ever seen. She is a truly gentle giant who is perfectly satisfied to eat and do nothing more. Sometimes she has to, though. She could knock down the barn, or me, heaven knows, if she felt like it, but that isn't the way she is. She loves to be hand fed—things like carrots and apples. When she decides to do some relatively high-speed laps around the pasture or when she comes running up to see what goodies you have brought, the ground shakes and you can hear the thunder in the house some distance away.

TJ is a Standardbred who won the Ohio Stakes as a trotter. A sweeter-mannered "easy keeper" you will never meet. She will go as willingly under saddle as in front of a cart. She is, as they say, biddable. She is just a very nice, mellow horse and is still this side of ten. Sometimes she feels like running and cuts loose, heels high and head into the wind. The other horses look at her in amazement, but no one seems to mind. She settles down soon enough and joins in the munching.

Something of a mystery is SHERRY. We know her to be three-quarters Arab and one-quarter Saddlebred, yet she is flawlessly dressed out as a Palomino! Since neither Arabs nor Saddlebreds throw Palomino colors, as far as I know, where did that design come from? She is really lovely and very sweet. When she doesn't feel like being restrained it is impossible for an adult to get a lead line on her, but a child can. She stands still when our grandchildren approach and lets them hook her up and lead her in. She is a very soft horse.

CHRISTY is a horse. She is, though, purebred. There is no mule or kangaroo in her. She is pure horse and although quiet and pleasant in the pasture and well mannered in the barn, she is a positive pain when the leather is in place. It takes a really very good rider to handle her, but even they go off. She likes dumping people. I suppose she thinks it is funny. Why keep an eating machine nobody likes to ride? It is hard to say, but where would she go? Who but us would have her? No horse of mine is ever going to become dog food or work in a hack stable for idiots to kick to pulp. No, Christy the pain can hang out.

HUMBOLDT is Maggie's love, the tall, handsome stranger from a high and distant land. Humboldt is a llama whose folks came from the Andes, probably Peru or Ecuador. He is really splendid, light chocolate brown with a white-and-black face. He comes from an excellent background and is haughty as all get-out, but he doesn't bite and only rarely spits. He did kick Karen Dorn, our farm manager, when he got his rabies shot. Both Karen and Humboldt went straight up in the air when the needle hit, six legs akimbo. Karen looked surprised all spread out like that in the manure, but Humboldt continued looking haughty. In his estimation he had acted perfectly appropriately. *You stick me, I kick you and then things can go back to normal. Show me another needle and I'll kick your butt again. You are better off giving me carrots.* It makes sense, if you think about it. At least from a llama's point of view.

Until we got all of the routines worked out, we used to put cat food on the back porch, up high where the dogs couldn't get at it. Jean Valjean and his mother were always on hand when we came down the driveway; if it was raining they would be just inside the barn doors, ready to race ahead of us to be there and point out that their dish was empty, with pitiful mewing. When we brought food out to them they would do their ankle-twining thing. Now Jean Valjean gets fed in the barn and in the kennel kitchen, as the new little gray cat will if it stays around. (It has!) The minute Karen or Pam arrives the lying starts. *"I'm starving. I haven't been fed in days—help, help, help."*

Karen does what I have not been able to do. She can squat down and pat Jean Valjean with no adverse

reaction. "But no picking up," Karen says, "just patting." Ask Jill about that.

For a tom, even an altered tom, Jean Valjean has not been a wanderer. With his mother gone, he is still hanging out here. The new kitten may prove another

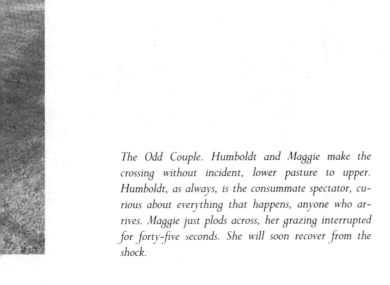

The Odd Couple. Humboldt and Maggie make the crossing without incident, lower pasture to upper. Humboldt, as always, is the consummate spectator, curious about everything that happens, anyone who arrives. Maggie just plods across, her grazing interrupted for forty-five seconds. She will soon recover from the shock.

anchor. The black-and-white stranger Jean Valjean was on safari with yesterday? With food and water and shelter and an ongoing zoological sideshow to entertain them, why should any fixed cat want to stray?

Old Scar-Marked Teddy near the Orchid Greenhouse.
He expects trouble but never gets it. I think he is
disappointed because it is so peaceful. The streets of
San Francisco were never like this.

7

Siafu

EVERY NOW AND THEN there is one very special animal that crosses over the bridge in a way that is truly magical. That bridge, of course, is the one that spans the chasm that naturally exists between our species and all others. Animal people—animal lovers (why not?)—try to cross that bridge as often as possible. Some few individual animals make it easy, or at least a great deal easier. They come more than halfway. They reach out as we reach out and we succeed in touching each other.

What made Siafu so special? I am not sure. He was the only one of his litter that we kept. That could be part of it. He was clearly the runt, and he was somehow injured when he was a day or two old and developed a large abscess in his right shoulder. He started out being needy and perhaps that had something to do with his special appeal. He needed a nurturing family, and he had one. We were all well matched at the outset.

The infected pocket that went all the way to the joint required flushing with a syringeful of saline solution every few hours and therefore entailed a great deal of handling. When the infection was finally defeated by large doses of antibiotics—Siafu would have a limp and a strange toe-out gait for the rest of his life—Jill and my mother-in-law, Phyllis, were determined to make the tiny kitten into the most highly socialized cat of all time. They did it, in fact, with the entire litter. They took turns. The kittens were held, stroked, carried, touched and touched and touched some more. It worked. They were all incredible cats. Siafu, "Little Biting Ant" in Swahili, was soon the only one left. People continued to remark about the others a decade later. Each was "the most remarkable cat I have ever known." It was simply a matter of intense, deliberate socialization. I am convinced it can be done with any domestic cat, if the holding and petting starts on its first day of life. The natural condition for that cat becomes intense human contact.

Xnard Watching Jean Valjean Acting Beguilingly. It isn't really submission, as far as I can tell, but it is a peace signal of some kind. It is rather like saying, "Here is my soft underside and my exposed throat—I offer them to you as proof of my trust." I don't think cats think quite that way or handle abstractions all that well, but genetically that is what appears to be going on.

Siafu (and this is true of his littermates as well) had something else going in his favor. He was an American Shorthair Silver Ash tabby, and wearing that name requires very specific "beauty" points. On his sides he had perfect bull's-eye targets, concentric diminishing circles of silver and black. (Inexplicably, as he got older, that jet black lightened into a lustrous dark brown and even that was changing toward a kind of reddish gold as a wash on the longest hairs when he died.) On his throat he had three unbroken strands of beads, black on silver. On the front of his forehead there was a perfect M and on the back of his neck an equally perfect butterfly. Crossbandings on his forelegs completed his distinctive markings and added up to a perfectly beautiful cat. He had a round, intense little face, and as his initial runt status predicted he never did grow to be very large. He got rounder as he got older, but he remained a small and very huggable cat, who loved to be hugged. As soon as he was picked up he went limp. Clearly he loved it and was wholly at ease. No question, Siafu with his sweet temper and splendid good looks made everybody love him.

The little tabby made the transition from East Hampton to Thistle Hill Farm with no problem at all. He was so people-oriented that anything was fine with him as long as his people were at hand. After the required indoor imprinting period, he began to explore outside with the rest of the curious crew, and curious they truly were. But he was at the back door asking to come in before sundown every day. He was more than imprinted; it was as if he were attached to the house and his family by a bungee cord.

Eventually the widening rings of exploration he was making around the house included the barn, and he spent a part of each day, as far as we know, with Cosette and Jean Valjean. Since he and Jean Valjean were both males (even though both were neutered) there was a brief ceremonial standoff with some halfhearted spitting. It was strictly pro forma. Siafu was a dream of a cat, a true pussycat, but he was never a wimp. The big-man-on-campus nonsense never amounted to anything. Siafu became, by all odds, the handsomest part-time barn cat anyone ever saw. Unlike the Siamese ladies, he was not a snob.

Siafu loved dogs, and any one of ours that plopped down for a rest was sure to have Siafu arching and rubbing under its chin and marking it with the glands at the corners of his mouth. The purring was intense. He curled up with any dog at hand. And when one of the younger dogs decided to maul him he just rolled over and the more drool the dog deposited on his coat the louder Siafu purred. I worried about him. He was so absolutely trusting he was vulnerable. Clearly he never believed that anyone or anything in this world would hurt him. Happily he was not to be betrayed. Nothing visible ever did.

We never knew Siafu's Thistle Hill beat to go any further than the barn. He would swing by there, visit with Cosette and his pal Jean Valjean (for the two males —they were apparently about the same age—did become friends), and then it was back down toward the house. As far as we know he didn't go back as far as the woods, nor was he ever seen going to or from the

streams. I saw him at the edge of the marsh directly behind the house, but never I never saw him in it or on any other side of it.

In the house he liked time on the windowsill or one of the banquettes in the kitchen. That is the center of activities, as is any country kitchen. That's where the macaws' very large cages are and the human traffic. Somebody is always asking somebody if they would like a cup of coffee or tea, and the kitchen table is where it

Friends for Life. Lizzie (foreground) is showing her age. She is about ten now. Old animals are especially nice, I think. They have a kind of inexplicable wisdom, a resignation, somehow. Guy de Windrows (pronounced Gee with a hard G) is a Petit Basset Griffon Vendéen or PBGV. These two "hang out" and have for years. They understand each other. They would like to run as fast as the sight hounds but understand that they can't.

all happens. Ninety-five percent of our meals are taken in the kitchen rather than in the dining room. And that all suited Siafu perfectly.

Siafu never bit anyone and never scratched anyone intentionally. That is normal for a well-adjusted pet. But he went far beyond not committing negative acts, he wallowed in the positive act of loving. He was wonderful with our grandchildren even when they each in turn went through the uncivilized year between roughly two and three. We stopped any mauling as soon as it was detected, but however much of it there was he tolerated, and purred.

To say that Siafu *never* had his doubts about another animal is not quite true. Friend Vicki Croke, an ace writer-journalist with the *Boston Globe,* frequently travels with her dog, Lacy. Naturally, she expects a big welcome for her pet here. Everyone does. I'll wager that if a member of either the Anheuser or the Busch family came to stay they'd bring eight or ten Clydesdales with them.

Vicki is not a large lady, not at all. In fact she is rather on the diminutive side. That makes it a little difficult to explain Lacy who, although a dog, is the size, approximately, of a Bactrian camel. Lacy is a true giant, an Irish Wolfhound. It can be fun to try to analyze people and their pets. What in this animal appeals to that person? It is very obvious in some cases such as the closet wimp who avails himself of an attack-trained Rottweiler as an extension of an imagined self. But Vicki and the Hound of the Baskervilles! In fact, Lacy is a very sweet dog, sweet and vulnerable, but big, big-time, industrial-strength big.

The first time Vicki brought "the moose" down to Thistle Hill was, I think, something of a shock for poor Siafu. We were in the kitchen about to have coffee and try to decide how Vicki could have possibly misinterpreted my flawless instructions on how to get here from Boston. There was no room for Lacy to stretch out on the kitchen floor and retain the freezer and refrigerator, not to mention the stove, so she was banished to the hall just outside the kitchen door. Siafu had apparently been sleeping upstairs and heard the rise in volume Vicki's arrival elicited. (It is perfectly natural for sound level to go up when people are arriving or departing.)

Lacy was spread out like a shaggy nine-by-twelve-foot rug at the foot of the stairs when Siafu came down to get in on the good stuff going on in the kitchen. On the last step he suddenly became aware of the new dog and stepped down for a little sniffing and perhaps even some snuggling. Lacy was not conditioned to cats and was not sure whether she was supposed to ignore them, salute them, or eat them. She stood up slowly, never taking her eyes off Siafu.

Siafu watched in utter amazement as the largest creature he would probably ever see bearing the dog smell opened like an extension ladder. His eyes seemed to get wider (they probably didn't) and you could almost hear him wheez, "Holy s———!!!" before he let loose with one loud yowl, shot between Lacy's legs, and vanished back up the stairs with Lacy staring after him in amazement. For the rest of her stay Siafu stalked Lacy one floor up, moving from rail post to rail post, peering down and trying to keep the monster in view. I am sure it was nothing more than a game. On her second visit some months later, Siafu apparently forgave Lacy her size and walked through the gray redwood forest of her legs without concern.

As would appear obvious, Siafu was a very contented cat. He could make a game of something unusual like Lacy's obscene size. In fact it almost seemed as if he had a flair for the dramatic. He probably would have been a leading man if he had been human. He was pleased by physical contact as he had been conditioned to be since his first day among us. (He was born in a box in our bedroom. That's among us.) Everything about life pleased him immensely.

He was about ten when feline leukemia struck. He was one of the three the serum somehow did not protect. One life form that Siafu's handsome good looks and wonderful disposition could not charm was a virus, and that is what causes leukemia in cats. Along with Cosette and Fluffy Louise he suddenly stopped eating. In a day his coat looked rough and out of condition. He was listless and ran a fever. His nose and his eyes had discharges and when there was only one thing left to do, we did it.

I guess multiple pet owners really shouldn't have favorites any more than parents should. But that is a theoretical state of purity I have not been able to achieve when considering animals. I have had favorites among our animals, lifetime favorites, and Siafu was at the top of my cat list with perhaps two or three others.* I have

---

* *The others were Rufus, an incredible hybrid—domestic cat and bobcat cross—Daisy, a fey little fluffy cat with a personality not unlike Siafu's, who used to stand up on her hind legs and tap me when she wanted attention, which she nearly always did. Good Lord, how that little cat liked to eat! I guess Abigail would be the other. She was a lovely Seal-Point Siamese we bought when we lived in London. The one time we lost her was when she was a kitten. We*

probably had close to fifty cats in my life, so the top three or four rank high indeed. There never will be a time when I can think of Siafu and not miss him. Together we crossed that bridge and we met somewhere near the middle.

---

found her after a hysterical half hour such as Hampstead Heath had not seen before (or since) inside a guitar owned by the children's nanny. Perhaps it is a toss-up between Abigail and another equally lovely Siamese named Thai Lin——the baby-sitter. We got her in New York. There have been so many, and each was in its own way special.

Xnard Determined to Stay Neat and Clean. A former drug addict (that was forced on him by some whacked-out college students in Boston), Xnard is determined to keep himself in reasonable shape despite the weight of his many years. He always has been a really nice cat with a perfectly feline take on materialism. He hangs in at Thistle Hill, and the other animals seem to respect him, somehow. Anthropomorphic, yes, but there is some sense to the idea.

8

Xnard

XNARD (PRONOUNCED SNARD) has appeared from time to time in other cat books that I have written *(A Celebration of Cats, A Cat Is Watching)*, but forgive me that. I am very fond of him, and if you already know a little about him, look upon him as I do. He is an old friend. After all, when reading a book or seeing a newscast it is kind of nice to know something about what is being reported. It is insider stuff.

Xnard was a former involuntary drug addict. Some "heads" at Boston University, where Clay was both a premed and medical student, were feeding Xnard and his littermate LSD. Xnard's brother apparently decided he was a cockatoo or lorikeet or something else feathered, because he took off from a tenth-story windowsill and didn't make it. One of the great fictions about cats —and there are so many nonsense tales one has to be pretty rich to be labeled "great"—is that cats can fall from almost any height and land on their feet uninjured. If you believe that one I would like to show you a statue of a lady in New York Harbor I might be willing to sell.

Cats are pretty good at adjusting midair descent paths and impact angles, but a cat dropped from a considerable height will be killed just as surely as your aunt Minnie and your good ol' dog Tray would be. Xnard's brother was killed, but fortunately he was probably so out of it at the time he surely thought he really was flying, and the impact killed him instantly.

At any rate, medical student Clay visited the drug den (in a college dorm) and sold the druggies on the idea that it would be better if Xnard went home with him rather than have them go out the window, too, in search of Xnard's brother.

The young medical student, although not yet in clinical rotations, prescribed cold turkey—i.e., instant and total withdrawal from anything stronger than tuna fish. Even catnip was ruled out. No highs for Xnard, no soporifics. To the best of my knowledge the little gray-and-white cat—he never grew to be very large—has never craved anything but the odd bit of beef or lamb slipped to him as a supposedly forbidden table scrap.

Xnard today is in his teens, middle teens, and that makes him, reckoning on averages, a pretty old cat. I have always adored puppies and kittens with their milky baby breath. I love young foals—hell, I like young'uns of any kind, even our own. (I am categorically certifiable about our grandchildren.) As I have added the years onto my own back, though, I find myself more and more drawn to older animals. I feel about them, I guess, the way they feel about me at that stage. It is old-shoe time. We fit; we're comfortable with each other; we've shared most of our secrets with each other.

That gray on an older animal's muzzle should be purple (for the Purple Heart). The old-timers, for the most part, have been through one kind of wringer or another. They have the scars to prove it and they are just asking for a little of the good stuff before they head for the big Kitty Litter box (or kennel run) in the sky. Although we don't ask for it from any animal we encounter, the old-timers do seem to be grateful. We have both grizzle-faced dogs and cats, and I love them especially. If they come over and ask to be petted, it is with a certain wisdom: *"Hey, I am going to love this, and it will be good for your blood pressure, too."* And they'll be right.

Xnard is like that, a venerable senior citizen who quite properly feels it is his time for cushions. He doesn't like to feel cold, and he wants things to be soft and relatively unexciting. He still likes a good mystery, he loves to be curious about something, but enough of the old rough-and-tumble. Quiet mysteries are just fine. His hips and wrists are probably as good at predicting lousy weather as mine are. (I would like to be able to explain to near geriatrics like Xnard that if you are human, at least, and you are over fifty in our years, and you wake up in the morning and nothing hurts—you're dead. The same, on their time scale, is true of cats and dogs, I am sure, but how ever would you let them know that?) I like seeing old-timers like Xnard get what they want. It just feels right.

I don't know how long Xnard is going to last. He is slowing down. Four years ago or so when we first took over here, Xnard was into deep, penetrating exploration. On the far side of our densest stand of woods there is a very, very large pasture that descends a steep slope and ends up at the same stream that runs right past the house. We lease that pasture to an adjoining horse farm, and they use it variously for mares or stallions. It is a fair walk back through the woods, but we do go back there looking for wildflowers in three seasons and the sledding slope for the kids in winter. On more than a few occasions a few years ago we emerged into the clearing, and there would be Xnard, back alone with seven or eight of our neighbor's horses. He had to have gone along the stream bank, across the marsh, or skirted the marsh to the south and cut through the woods further up the slope that is common to the woodland as well as the big pasture beyond.

I guess he must have hunted back there. There are all kinds of wild things, and he had it all to himself. I have seen Lilly the Greyhound back that far, but never another of our cats. Some strangers from time to time, but Xnard was the only Thistle Hill Regular.

Xnard doesn't go through the woods anymore. If it was the hunting that attracted him, that activity has lost its charm for him. I think it is just too long a walk. He seems to like things closer to home now. He does go up to the barn and visit with Jean Valjean.

•

BULLETIN . . . Flash from the barn, word just in. The new little gray job is still with us. Pam Holder has seen it again. It is evidently eating at the communal barn cat (plus guests from the main house) bowl. Still looks unkempt, the latest intelligence reports state, and it appears to be all gray, as the earlier bulletin stated. It is very shy and is going to be hard to trap. Karen and Pam can do it, though. I have nothing but faith. It has to be trapped, because whether it stays or moves on it is going to be unable to reproduce. That is a condition, you will recall, for eating and gaining shelter at Thistle Hill Farm. And shots —I still have faith in them despite our recent heavy loss. It has to have rabies protection, certainly, and all of the other shots, too, including feline leukemia. It shall be done. But if it is this frightened at such an apparently early age, it probably won't be as good as Omari at negotiating life's sharper corners. Still, the barn loft with all those hay caves isn't a bad life. It beats alleys and gutters and junked cars and there is lots of action here, more than enough to keep a curious cat occupied. Back to Xnard . . .

•

One thing I notice about Xnard is what appears to be periodic reverie. He will be walking along, usually outside, and he will stop. He will stand as still as a garden ornament with his head just slightly down and seem to be listening. He will be lost in thought, or so it would seem, but that would be difficult to prove at this stage in our knowledge of animal cognition. Cats think, surely, because they solve problems, but "lost in thought" would be something else. It would mean that Xnard is capable of such consuming abstractions that for moments or minutes he could attend to them alone detaching himself from the immediate world to do it. I don't think that is likely, but, we must remember, when I say "I think" there isn't a person alive who can tell me what that really means. We don't know how we think, so when we get to animal cognition at a level as high as Xnard's, our confusion is monumental. We need a good dose of humility. We have to be able to say in all truth, "We don't know yet," and live with it. It may be a long time before we know what we are doing when we think or what it would feel like not to think or to think like someone else. We are, after all, locked away from each other, not to mention our cats. We can't get into their minds any more than we can each other's.

Jill and I have been married thirty-nine years, and we went together for three years before that. In the majority of situations I can pretty well predict how she will react to something just as she can foresee my behavior. That is because we have four decades of accumulated empirical evidence to base our educated guesses on. Still, we surprise each other all the time.

Now take Xnard—or any other cat, for that matter. Without any experience whatsoever with their sen-

Emmy's Eyes. What have they seen, what is behind them that we may never know? What have cats always known that is lost to us? Look into their eyes and try to guess. Sometimes they look back and sometimes they don't. They are passageways to a mind that we may never be able to negotiate, although "never" is really a very long time. It will, though, take telepathy. Almost certainly that is so.

sory package, without knowing what it is like to receive the data their brain receives from however many senses they actually have, and without the foggiest notion of how or *what* they think, how could we predict their behavior? Only in a few relatively fixed, easily stage-managed situations can we do so. If a strange cat comes on campus it may be ignored or it may be chased away. I don't know which it will be, and I don't know why. I have no idea what signals cats are giving each other,

Martha Custis Washington Thinks Things Through. Under a favorite bush she is in repose and just watches the world go by. There are so many things to see at Thistle Hill that if there is such a thing as boredom in animals, it doesn't happen here. They amuse each other and they often follow each other to see what is going to happen next.

what challenges are being offered. Cats still have their own world safe from our prodding and probing. It is one of the most confounding things about living with animals and one of the most profoundly interesting. We can watch them function, we can call some few shots in advance, again from accumulated empirical evidence,

but we can't figure out why. We can't even begin to figure out why.

As affectionate as our cats are and as trusting as cats like my old, long-gone friend Daisy and, more recently, Siafu were, there is one strange hesitation every cat I can remember exhibits. Siafu was a little glutton,

and Daisy was absolutely devoted to food as no other
cat I have ever known. If you put a dish of anything
from dry cat chow to milk in front of them they dived in
without a moment's hesitation. Offered food by fingers,
though, and they sniffed and thought about it and sniffed
again. They acted as if you were trying to poison them!

Dogs, heaven knows, lunge for food offered, but
not cats, not when it is offered by fingers. I have never
quite understood why that is so. Cats, like dogs, have a
good sense of smell, and Xnard uses it to an almost
absurd degree. Offer him the choicest morsel and he
will turn his head slightly and sniff and sniff and sniff.
*"Trying to slip a little of that old arsenic on me, are you? Not
this time you don't."* It has gone on to such an absurd
length of time that on occasion, I must confess, I have
withdrawn the offer.

Perhaps having one or two pets is different from
having thirty or so as we do—I mean in other than the
obvious ways. We don't view Xnard or any of the other
denizens of Thistle Hill Farm as cogs or faceless members of a crowd. We still treasure every one and recognize their different needs and contributions. Their
interactions with each other are instructive, rewarding,
and entertaining. I try to recall the times I, or Jill and I
together, had one pet or two and it doesn't seem we
loved them more than we do individual members of
our gang now. Perhaps memory fails me; perhaps it is
substantively different. I really can't say for certain, but
it seems to me not.

The way we can anticipate death or deal with it

when it comes: Is that a function of our being older and more familiar with it or is it a function of numbers? Is it easier to lose one of thirty than it is one of one or two? I don't know, but I do know that I can realize that Xnard is failing, that he is slowing down, without the hysteria some pet owners suffer when time is closing in on them. I know. For years I have been hearing regularly from friends and strangers about the horrors of death. I have cried, too; I have felt a brick replace my heart and threaten to strangle me. But now, I realize, in a quiet and I guess resigned way, that every pet we ever hold is a tragedy waiting to happen to us. It is inevitable. Besides, from long experience I know that the fact that a pet dies is far less important than that it lived. I can look back on some lifetime favorites like Rufus and Daisy, on Yankee the Bloodhound and Brigitte the Toy Poodle, and I smile inside, not cry. I remember the wonderful things they used to do, not when they stopped doing them. And that is the way I feel about Xnard. We have had about a decade and a half of his deliberate, dour, but tolerant ways. He is as familiar to us as we are to each other, and although it is hard to think of what life will be like then, we can be sure that there will be life after Xnard. I guess the only question we have to ask is, did we do as well by him as we could have? I hope the answer is yes. I think it is.

Mr. Sweetface Himself—Topy the Golden Whippet. One of the very sweetest creatures on this green earth. He is a tough little farm bum at heart but generous in his dealings with other animals and a cat lover from the moment he met his first one, Emmy, in the back seat of our car. Emmy managed to get out of her carrier and Topy woke up with Emmy sitting on him. He looked, seemed to shrug and say, "Oh, so you're what a cat is," and went back to sleep.

9

Like Cats and Dogs

IF THE STORY of the Thistle Hill Regulars proves nothing else it should finally put to rest the expression *"They fought like cats and dogs."* That is one of those concepts based on partial, ancient truths that gets jammed into a folklore without the benefit of analysis and hangs there resisting all sense and all evidence that might prove it wrong or at least modify it. By the sheer power of repetition, like propaganda or a political slogan, it assumes the aura of fact. But aura isn't evidence and fact requires rather more support than propaganda. Thus, in time, fiction becomes conventional wisdom, but conventional wisdom is seldom as wise as its name would seem to imply.

The facts are that the ancestors of our dogs, and of our cats, too, were dedicated hunters. They still exist in their original forms, and they are still hunters working their respective habitats over for all they are worth. That means that they were and are as wild species fairly intolerant of each other. They are competitors, frequently after the same prey and the same serendipitous carrion. They also both like the same kind of cover where they can bear and raise their young. But when they are nearly matched in size it probably is a survival advantage for them to leave each other alone. No, not probably; it *is* a survival advantage.

Nature frequently does that, gives animals escape routes, white flags to wave to ward off fang-and-claw encounters. A mountain lion/wolf fight, although some producers might think it would make a terrific scene in a "nature" movie, would profit neither animal nor either species. Numbers can substitute for bulk, as with lions versus African hunting dogs in Africa. No five-hundred-pound lion, powerful as it is—and it *is* powerful—wants to tangle with six or eight sixty-pound African hunting dogs.

In nature the trick is not to win over another animal. That is a last resort when nothing else works. The goal is to survive (which usually means you are made of the right stuff) and reproduce. If that can be done without bloodshed not related to hunting, so much the better. Our own species is so bewilderingly violent that we constantly seek any hint of violence in nature to justify, perhaps, or explain ourselves. It is a fool's errand. We can neither explain nor justify how people who love Mozart can murder and maim, how people who appreciate Monet can rape babies, how people who value fine wine can engage in genocide. It really is a shame that as a footnote we try to protest, *"See, cats and dogs are like that, too."* But there is an enormous difference between getting dinner and having fun.

Dogs—wolves—indeed evolved as chasers with a pursuer's speed and stamina, and when something runs within their sight some dogs can be trigger-happy just as some cats can be. It is natural for dogs to chase, and our dogs are generally larger than our domestic cats. The results can indeed be catastrophic.

All that would seem to support that old conventional wisdom of domestic dogs and cats inevitably being at each other's throats. But that in turn would ignore the undeniable fact of domestication and all it entailed. Both dogs and cats have been changed dramatically by millennia of selective breeding, cats over the last four thousand years and dogs over an incredible time span of between fifteen and twenty thousand years. It is difficult to overstate the changes that much manipulation by purposeful selection can foster. Look at a Great Dane, a Chihuahua, a Bulldog, an Irish Setter, and a Shih Tzu. They are exactly the same species, manipulated into those specialized forms by unrelenting selection. Differences in behavior brought about by the same interference are hardly less dramatic.

Earlier we discussed how cats have had to surrender that precious solitude built into every feline species except the lion, in order for them to fit into the style of living we have designed for ourselves and all the life forms that we control. I believe a demand has been made on both cats and dogs to coexist for exactly the same reason, to fit in with us. It isn't all that unreasonable a demand if you think about it: *"You guys can live with us and we'll pick up the tab, if you will only stop killing each other. And stop the noise!!"*

Dogs are wonderful hot-water bottles, and cats, once they have gotten the word, love to snuggle up with them. Now that Alice has come around, almost every cat here except Teddy (and he shows no difference at all in his attitude toward dogs and his approach to almost all cats) picks a dog at nap time or for the night and nestles in.

Lilly the Greyhound almost always has a cat and frequently holds it in her front paws as the two friends wash each other's face and ears. It really is lovely to watch, but in at least a couple of ways it represents our domination over both species. We took them from the wild, we molded them by baby-sitting their genes and forced them into entirely new patterns of behavior. That is not a negative statement, but at least let's recognize what is going on under our noses.

There is a chaise lounge in the top-floor sitting

A Common Reptile at Thistle Hill Farm——a Lounge Lizard. Sirius or Xyerius was scheduled to die because he had stopped winning at the track. He was two and a half then, not exactly old! He doesn't look it in this, one of his favorite poses, but he is still a wonderful athlete. As soon as it is cool, he does laps, lots of them, over about an acre and a half of lawn. He moves at more than thirty to thirty-five miles an hour and then heads back to the lounge. He is extremely gentle and accommodating and loves cats.

room here at the farm, and I have been doing a some-what casual census of who is sleeping there. Every critter in the place seems to love it. My notes show: *Omari,* Lilly and Topaz; Lilly and *Alice;* Xyerius, *Alice* and *Mary Todd Lincoln;* Topaz and *Xnard;* Topaz, Xyerius and *Xnard;* and *Omari, Alice* and Reggie. A census in our bedroom shows the same pattern, only there are usually more animals because there is a king-size bed. The average is two cats and two to three dogs. In any room open ad lib to animals it is the same. That is, of course, as long as Teddy, America's favorite male single-parent mother, is not there. The banquettes in the kitchen are usually the same way: dog, cat, person, cat.

We have never had a real cat-and-dog fight, not in thirty-nine years. Considering the number of cats and dogs involved, that must be some kind of record. We did have a catastrophe, though, and a really terrible time was had by all. It was a nightmare we shared in broad daylight. We had a Bulldog named Pudge who loved cats. She was *really* a hot-water bottle and our cats loved her right back. But Pudge, as her name implies (we got her in London where her real name, her kennel name, was Glynis Gay Girl), had a fondness for food that was without boundaries. It was monumental, in fact. For Pudge, insane gluttony was moderation. She was the Henry VIII of the hydrant set. She inhaled food; she worshiped it; her enthusiasm knew absolutely no limits.

On one occasion someone dropped a bit of some-thing edible on the floor. I don't even remember what it was. Pudge and a new kitten arrived at the tidbit at the same time. Pudge snapped in reflex to assert her prior right to anything that was comestible. Her jaws were like a bear trap. The kitten died, its skull crushed. Clay and Pamela were young then, seven and ten, as I recall, and they both witnessed the whole thing. It was really bad for a while.

It was very difficult to explain to the children why they should not hate Pudge, that she didn't mean to really harm the kitten. How do you explain an animal's reflexive protection of food? The kids loved Pudge and saw the terrible thing they had witnessed as a betrayal. They were ambivalent, confused, and enormously saddened.

Pudge went to live with a lion and tiger trainer in Hollywood, and survived a full ten years, which has to be considered pretty good longevity for that breed. (Bulldogs are dwarfed Mastiffs and although no longer giants themselves, they share the Mastiff's short life span, as do all giant dogs.) She was a fantastic dog, a super, funny personality, but you never know when someone is going to drop a crumb or two. That is not what I would call a dog-and-cat fight. It was an accident. It is somewhat like smoking in bed. It is not arson, but a lot of people have died because someone else did it. What saddens me now is that I can't even remember the kitten's name. She had only been with us a few days, less than a week certainly. And then she died.

We have no misgivings about our cats and dogs together, inside the house or out. Aside from that one ugly accident with Pudge, we have never had anything

like an actual fight. Any new dog that even looks inquiringly at a cat gets shouted down immediately. Dickens, the black Greyhound puppy, thought cats would be fun to chase. We didn't even get to complete his correction course. He tried it with Fluffy Louise, who landed a fistful of claws on his nose and made a sharp, explosive sound to go with the corrective gesture. Dickens got the message. He is fine with cats. Even when he had the not terribly bright idea of chasing them, his intention, I am

Are You for Real? Guy checks out a dog without odor, a gift newly arrived from Gump's in San Francisco, a gift from Rich Avancino, president of the SFSPCA. Anything new on the farm has to be checked out by every dog and every cat before it can be truly accepted as part of the scene. This figure was sniffed by nine cats and twelve dogs before they arrived at a consensus. It offers nothing of interest to them. It won't play or respond in any way and it isn't comfortable or chewable. These are legitimate yardsticks.

sure wasn't blood, but fun. After all, no puppy or kitten ever stopped to ponder the possible consequence of a good romp. That is, not until they had been imprinted with an unforgettable experience.

•

BULLETIN . . . My desk overlooks the marsh and beyond it the "deer yard" where I saw six deer the other day. I saw some movement out there a few moments ago and used my binoculars, which are never far away. Jean Valjean is sitting out there in the deer yard, where there are no deer in evidence at the moment. It is the strangest sight. Not only is it the first time I have seen him that far from the barn, all the way over at the edge of the woods, but he is not alone. A handsome cock pheasant is pecking around not three feet away from him. The pheasant is obviously ignoring Jean Valjean, but Jean Valjean is apparently fascinated with what "big bird" is doing. I can just imagine what is going through his evil little mind: "If only I were three pounds heavier. I wonder. Do I dare?" "Big bird" seems to be convinced he doesn't. It is a strange thing to watch! I assume that if any deer show up to nap or browse both the pheasant and himself will split. We'll watch.

•

Introducing cats to each other, even when they are not really neurotic about it like Teddy, is a more difficult challenge than mixing cats with dogs. Actually, Teddy is the only failure I can recall and I still have hope. Alice still doesn't like other cats very much, but she doesn't attack them, she ignores them with haughty grandeur and now obviously has discovered dogs.

The art of introducing new cats to an existing feline population is not brain surgery, it is common sense. Watch—above all else, watch—and be prepared to step in only if you are really needed.

Since reaching into a real screaming cat brawl can be like grabbing a spinning circular saw, it is a good idea to have interceders other than your own flesh handy if you anticipate its really being needed. A heavy-duty spray bottle with a mild ammonia solution or even an aerosol can of room air freshener will serve, but only when someone is going to get hurt. Anything but your bare hands. Cats have a very sensitive nose, and that is an advantage for them. It also can be a management tool for you to exploit when the situation is extreme.

As for spitting, growling, and hissing, they are all natural and can be anticipated and pretty much ignored. A great many people overreact to that kind of natural display. Posturing doesn't require intercession. Cats may be readily socialized because they have yielded to domestication, but that doesn't mean they won't grumble about it. We applaud the fact that our cats purr and smooch to express their pleasure. It is hardly fair to deny them their right to the opposite mood. Our own moods shift as we encounter different stimuli. Why shouldn't theirs?

•

BULLETIN FROM THE BARN . . . Karen just brought me the mail and reports that there is another new cat in the barn. This cat is apparently a well-rounded adult and appears not to be shy, rather a purrer and an ankle-rubber. The tiny gray kitten has not been seen in a few days, but that doesn't mean anything. It is very shy, and a new delivery of hay a few days ago might have frightened it into hiding. The maze in that loft, when hundreds of bales of hay are in place, is astounding because the bales are loosely stacked to allow air to circulate. A cat could hide out there for months and not be seen. It would just have to switch from diurnal movements to nocturnal, something a cat is perfectly able to do. This is an unusual time even for busy Thistle Hill. In a matter of a couple of weeks two cats of very different ages and apparently backgrounds have shown up and joined Jean Valjean in the barn. We may have to issue membership and ID cards so we can tell the Regulars from the transients! At

Weathered Wood Farm, just across the way, the Gentrys report four new cats in their barn during the same period. One can imagine that all of this could be coincidence, but it seems unlikely. It would not be the first time a rural area has had a mass dumping. All bad things to whoever is doing it.

•

As we have gone along, I've tried to dispel a few of the myths about cats. First, the utter nonsense about their being "no maintenance" pets. That is in no way true. Their food, their preventative medical schedule, and their spaying and neutering are not one whit less imperative than the same concerns in canine care. Although this household is no place for the statement to be issued, because, frankly, it is a matter of "practice what I preach not what I do," in almost all settings cats are far better off inside than outside.

In a town or city, certainly, and in the suburbs as well, wandering cats have short, unfortunately eventful lives. We live way out in the boonies precisely so we can have animals, wild and domestic, in a natural setting. For the reasons explained, strictly indoor cats would not be a manageable situation here. Unless a person is willing to have the supermarket, drugstore, post office, and dry cleaner a fifty-minute round trip away, they really shouldn't think of indoor-outdoor cats. My office is a ten-hour round-trip commute and requires my having a second residence for use when I am there during the week. It is a price I am willing to pay to have things the way we do here at Thistle Hill Farm.

Then there was the silly business about cats landing on their feet and being able to fall great distances and not be harmed. Remember Xnard's poor brother. Again, utter nonsense, yet people still believe it.

The third myth is the main subject of this chapter —dogs and cats being natural and intractable enemies. Patently, that is rarely even partially true with animals that have been socialized and conditioned for life in a human family. And that is what a cat should be, a part of a family. That is at least as true of dogs, too, obviously. Although we are extremely fond of them, our horses, cows, donkey, alpaca, and llama are somehow different. I guess coming in and out of the house is a kind of dividing line although once when he had made one of his frequent Houdini-like escapes, Steakums, our steer, did end up on the back porch peering in the kitchen window at us. Do you suppose he was telling us something? Of course, that was before he had Fat Susan Jane to keep him company. Since his affair started he hasn't shown any great need for our company unless food is involved. He will still accept offerings.

Myth number four: cats can't be trained. They can, if you are a control freak and into that kind of thing. I believe that cats are as intelligent as dogs and pigs. In my estimation they all have about the same potential. What separates their accomplishment levels is their personalities. What are they willing to learn or at least admit they have learned? That certainly is a factor, perhaps the main one. We don't even train our dogs here

at Thistle Hill except for basic obedience. We use a super dog trainer named Brian Kilcommons. He makes it look so easy.

There was a veterinarian in Connecticut years ago, Dr. George Whitney, who believed cats can be trained to do anything dogs can do except those things that lack of size and brute strength preclude. He had cats fetch-

*Rules of the Road at Thistle Hill Farm. Xyerius and
Mary Todd Lincoln have places to go and, I am sure,
things to do. They observe the rules of the turf: Unless
you have honest business to conduct, like snuggling and
mutual grooming, everybody go your own way and
mind your own business. Each of these two animals
knows the other is there, but they are assiduously ob-
serving the Regs.*

ing, jumping through hoops, coming on call, sitting, staying, the whole nine yards. He used positive reinforcement, as you might expect. (Punishment is out!) One of his cats, a huge orange tabby, came to live with us for a while, but although he was trained to obey commands he was a frigid bit of work. He wasn't equipped to be a pet at all. Dr. Whitney took him back.

If you want to test the hypothesis yourself, run a simple test. Take a treat that you know your cat will adore, liver or kidney, for example. Pick something with a good, high olfactory level, in other words something good and stinky. Offer it at no other time except to introduce it, and keep it in a distinctive container with a lid you can rattle. When the cat is in the kitchen take the container out of the refrigerator, rattle the lid in a specific way, and offer the open container for the cat to smell. When you have the cat's attention, go to a specific place and offer a little of the goody there. After a few test runs, if you have picked the right treat, your cat will appear whenever you rattle that lid. The cat has been trained to come on a set signal, because every time you perform the little ritual you are reinforcing the cat's behavior with a reward.

You will notice that the cat will inevitably come to *you* when it hears the lid rattle, not the feeding place. here you need a second person. When the cat comes to you *do not* reward it. Have your assistant trainer pick the cat up and carry it to the feeding place and keep it there until you get to it, and then offer the reward. In short order the second part of this sequence will be part of the routine. You can work alone and not offer the treat until you get to the spot, making the cat follow you there, but it will be a slower process. What you want is a cat that upon hearing a signal will go to a specific place and wait to be rewarded. Simple, but it does demonstrate two things: a cat can be trained, and you can train a cat. One thing without the other would be less satisfying.

There is the belief commonly held that cats (and dogs, too) become fat and lazy after they have been spayed. Simply put, that is not true. Surgery is not fattening; food is. Dogs and cats that have been spayed or neutered are under far less stress, and if you allow them to, they may tend to be sedentary. It isn't surgery, however, but the lifestyle you foster and the food you feed.

No, cats cannot see in the absence of light. "Dark" is a relative term. How dark is dark? When there is *no* light, a cat can't see any better than you can. When there is reduced light, it can see very much better than you can. No magic is involved, just anatomy. The cat's eyes are designed to maximize whatever light there is for obvious reasons—nocturnal hunting. Look at the size of your cat's eye in relationship to the size of its skull. Then look at your own. It is a matter of design.

I always loved the one about cats sucking the breath out of an infant. Sure they do, and I'm going to break the three-minute mile on my seventieth birthday. We did have a Siamese cat named Thai Lin who was madly fixed on Pamela from the day we brought her home from the hospital. Thai Lin would simply not be separated from the infant willingly. We eventually did have to put a screen door on the bedroom because we did not want the chubby cat jumping into the crib, perhaps landing on the baby and startling her. We would lift her into the crib, and she would snuggle Pamela as she was still doing nine years later. (She died when we were all living in England for a year.) No, no breath sucking has been recorded in this century, at least not in Maryland.

As for being the familiars of witches (about which we joked a bit earlier), that would have to be put into perspective. You can't believe in a witch's familiar without believing in a witch. If you do believe in witches, sure, why not go for it. I would hate to think that I had interfered.

As for black cats being bad luck, I don't think so. I read somewhere that was true in the fourteenth century in Albania. Perhaps so. Every black cat we have had was good luck. I don't think that bad-luck bit has been true since the Middle Ages, in central Europe.

Ailurophobia? The fear of cats, blind, unreasoning fear, is real enough. Jill is terrified of snakes; a guy I know, otherwise pretty rational, is turned to quivering jelly by the thought of a spider. A famous science fiction writer, despite his brilliant understanding of space (and time) travel, has to hold business meetings in the lobbies of office buildings he is so terrified of heights. Elevators? Forget it.

A fellow who worked for me was so terrified of

the idea of flying that he couldn't meet or see someone off at an airport. That made things difficult for him, because he was a Hollywood press agent. He had once had a nightmare about being at an airport and being ground-jacked, I guess, forced aboard a plant at gun-point. Why anyone would have done that to Sydney, I can't imagine. People go numb at the thought of closed spaces (claustrophobia), open spaces (agoraphobia), of all kinds of things. So why not cats? They are perfect for the role: secretive, contained, wide-eyed, athletic, glam-orous, and they have a whole body of legends already surrounding them.

Those of us who love cats are typically a little off the wall, and so are the people (like Hitler, Napoleon, and Alexander the Great) who hated them. Let's face it, cats bring out the best in us and the worst.

•

BULLETIN . . . I didn't see the cock pheasant fly out of the "deer yard," but I did see Jean Valjean come out like a shot. A minute or two later a doe and this year's fawn appeared as if by magic. So much for Jean Valjean the big-game hunter.

•

Marmalade. The protruding tongue is symbolic. I have never known a cat more intent on sampling life in everything it has to offer. She is enthusiastic about food, the dogs, and the other cats. The only thing she is really not all that taken with is the human species. One feels she will come around. Her kind usually does.

10

Fluffy Louise

FLUFFY LOUISE wasn't fluffy, and she didn't look like a Louise (Louises have a certain look about them, I have found), but to five-and-a-half-year-old Sarah she did, and so the name. It does seem to us that grandchildren should have the right to name incomings. We had our shot at it as kids, then our kids did in their turn. I think kids can relate even better to an animal whose name they created or at least helped create. (I know that in my case I can't sneer at any names the kids come up with. I laid some beauts on defenseless animals in my time; there was a perfectly rotten miniature poodle we called Tutu, heaven help us. Wasn't that cute! We had a sleek, lithe black cat with huge, slanting almond-shaped eyes I named Eartha Kat, and as a kid I had a lovely brown-and-white laboratory rat I called Fibrino-gen, Fibby for short. There were a great many more, I fear, momentary lapses in taste or judgment. There is a far side to all of us but only a few people like the great Gary Larson—and the late, great Charles Addams—created actual institutions to immortalize the phenomenon.) I digress here. I must, for I have nowhere else to tell this story:

Charles Addams and I were part of a five-man team who judged a charity pet show every July. It was held to raise money for an animal shelter called Bide-a-Wee. Charlie and I were doing best-in-show, trying to decide between the sweetest snake, the best-groomed Shetland pony, the best-tempered cat, a canary that wouldn't sing, the smartest dog, and various other smaller mammals and reptiles. The judging of a "show" like that is really quite simple. You make sure the top prizes (everybody gets something) are about evenly divided between boys and girls, white kids and black kids and Asian kids if there are any, skinny and fat kids; and special attention is paid to any youngster who obviously needs a boost. The supposed quality of the animals is not at issue.

Charlie whispered to me, *"I'd like to give first prize*

to that ugly little boy with the ugly little turtle. They look just
alike."

I pointed out that we really shouldn't do it, because the turtle was an eastern box turtle, a threatened
species that was locally endangered. It was illegal for the
ugly little boy to have it. Charlie thought for a moment;
then his face brightened, passing quickly from contem-
plation to enlightenment. *"If it really is illegal for him to
have it, let's give him first prize then hang him."* But I do
digress.

Fluffy Louise joined us on a walk one night on a
dark country lane and that was it. She fell in step with
us and would not be put off. We were her chosen, and
she did need some help. She was only between six and
eight months old but was coming to the end of a preg-
nancy, presumably her first. Her abdomen was distended
and as tight as a snare drum.

By noon the next day she was spayed (in her case
it was a gang abortion), had all of her shots, and was
resting comfortably. She passed her feline leukemia test,
so a couple of days later she was in the laundry for her
mandatory imprinting period, and in a week she was
working her way through the Regulars, making her
peace or agreeing to a standoff on a one-by-one basis.

There is no way of knowing what Fluffy Louise's
history might have been. When she pointed her paw at
us and said, *"Okay, you're it,"* she was in good overall
condition, and she was reasonably well socialized. Of
course, her previous owners, for such there surely had
been, given her easy way with people, had not bothered

to have her spayed (I will never understand that!) and when the inevitable happened it seems likely that they drove her to a dark country lane and dumped her (and her kittens thereby) to live or die as chance, dogs, foxes, great horned owls, cars, and pickup trucks would have it. Astounding.

Our veterinarians generally give us a break because of the volume of business we provide, because it is a good idea generally to be our vet, and because I am on the faculty and the Board of Overseers of the School of Veterinary Medicine at the University of Pennsylvania. I can take an animal with real troubles to Philadelphia, U Penn, where there are board-certified specialists and extremely sophisticated diagnostic tools. The organization I have the honor of heading, the ASPCA, the oldest humane organization in the Western Hemisphere, founded in 1866, has the very fine Bergh Memorial Hospital, which is the fourth-largest institutional veterinary hospital in the world.

In a word, veterinary care is accessible to us here at Thistle Hill Farm at any level we need, or, rather, our animals need. With all of that it still costs us between a hundred and a hundred and fifty dollars for every cat or dog that we take on. That is just to get them settled initially with an examination, surgery, tests, and shots. Then there is food and veterinary care for life. The dumpers, the abandoners are not only indifferent to the fate of the animals they have enjoyed up to the time of the dumping, they are saying, *"Here, kindhearted stranger, whoever you are, you take on my responsibility, you pay my bills."*

I don't like those people, not one bit. If I could get my hands on them, I'd like to send them in for the same surgery. With their ethics they shouldn't be allowed to reproduce, either. Bad manners and inhumanity, not to mention pea-sized mentalities, can be passed along. Another generation of that kind of behavior we can well do without.

The fate of an animal, or our involvement with it at Thistle Hill, shouldn't really be expressed as a matter of dollars and cents. We don't view it that way. We do what we want to do because it brings us joy to do it. We care about what happens to a Fluffy Louise. No one is holding a gun to our collective head.

Fluffy Louise was a strange cat. She died after I had started making notes for this book, one of the three cats that were failed by the feline leukemia shots. But for the couple of years she was here she had her own way of doing things and her own ideas about how things should work. She was a very definite personality. If she liked cats, they could lie beside her and eat out of a food dish, their heads thrust in beside hers, but if she didn't like a cat she would chase it up a tree if it got within twenty feet of her. She never was a big cat, but she was assertive.

When it came to dogs, Fluffy Louise lived off tribal memory. She, for one, was not about to forget the relationship her ancestors and theirs had had in the wild.

It had been a Mexican standoff then and that was the way it was to be with her now. She didn't attack dogs, nor they her, but they did understand that although you might end up napping on opposite ends of the same couch with her, no greater intimacy than that was invited or would be welcome. That was okay with the dogs. They could get their feline fix any time they wanted to without pushing it with the cranky F.L.

Fluffy Louise was fine with people, although she could be a little standoffish at times. When she wanted something—food, a little social grooming—then she was all purrs and nose pokes, but at other times she openly avoided direct contact. She appeared to be a cat caught between two distinctly different sets of imperatives. Although she was sociable at what I would consider a minimum acceptable level given the size and complexity of our animal community, she had an edge. Fluffy Louise was hard, and if such can possibly be implied of a cat, she was calculating. Many people have what I think is a mistaken impression of cats in general, that they are all users without any real feelings except for their own hedonistic materialistic demands. That seemed to be truer of Fluffy Louise than of any cat I have ever known. She was out for Number One and she knew exactly where the buttons were and when to push them. At sea she would have been the first one into the lifeboat and the first one to hold a press conference after the rescue. One did not adore Fluffy Louise as one would a Siafu or Omari or even geriatric Xnard; one understood Fluffy Louise. She was pretty, at times quite responsive, and at times a little pushy with other animals. She was essentially unremarkable.

But then came the dreaded plague. Fluffy Louise, a midway cat; Cosette, a far-out barn cat; and Siafu, as close an inner-circle creature as a cat can be all had to die. No distinctions were made. The virus just pointed and said, *"You, you, and you."*

I am glad we "rescued" Fluffy Louise from the dark country lane. In the process we prevented her litter from being born, and we gave her, a living creature, an opportunity to enjoy what life had been allotted. She was between two and two and a half when she died of leukemia, but at least she had lived the good life as long as she did live. That is better than millions of other cats get to do.

In the Greenhouse. Teddy (left) looking meaner'n spit while his "kid" Marmalade tries to look disgruntled, too. When the orchids are outside, this is their place and the photographer is an intruder. It is all an act on both their parts. One pat and either of them would be purring. Why cats enjoy bluffing when there is no need to I will never understand.

170

11

The Lure

of

Feathers

IT WILL COME as a surprise to few people that cats were among the world's first dedicated ornithologists. There were birds on earth ("dinosaurs with feathers") millions of years before the first clear evolutionary line that would lead to the family Felidae was etched into the expanding potential of the mammals. When true cats got here (it had been a very long trip, and a great many mistakes had been made, all of which had become extinct along the way), when the cats evolved as distinctly different animals from the other members of the order Carnivora—canines, weasels, hyenas, bears, raccoonlike animals, and mongooses—the birds were waiting, taunting, singing their little hearts out. They were then as they are now just about the most persistently noisy and therefore attention-attracting animals around. Their only challenge in strictly limited habitats would be frogs. Birds are ubiquitous. Think of a walk in the woods. Do you hear the raccoons, opossums, snakes, salamanders, woodrats, moose, beavers, muskrats, bobcats, and bears? No, you hear birds. Cats do too. With their ears they not only hear the music we hear, they hear the birds' movements. That may seem amazing, but it is true.

There are a number of things that make birds attractive to cats. Many of them were, back then as they are now, good to eat. With the recent discovery of a poisonous bird on New Guinea, the first one known, we have to wonder at least if other birds way back then, when the shape of the cat and its future were being elucidated, were also dangerous to touch, but either way most of them were, as they are now, not only harmless but helpless.

Cats evolved nowhere in the world where birds did not precede them. In few places like New Zealand, Australia (in neither place did cats evolve), Madagascar, Africa, and South America a few species of birds grew to absolutely gigantic sizes and were unapproachable.

They would have been able to stomp any cat into the turf with ease. Today's three-hundred-pound ostrich in Africa, a dangerous drop-kick artist for any predator to tangle with, is a runt-of-the-clutch chickadee compared to New Zealand's moa or Madagascar's elephant bird. In most places, though, most or all species of birds are vulnerable. In the nest and in early flight stages they are utterly without defense. Many species of cats climb, of course, and that puts birds even more squarely in harm's way. Cats, with good reason, have always studied birds with enormous self-interest.

Birds not only provide parcels of splendidly gift-wrapped food but are also exciting to cats because they trill, cheep, and chirp challengingly; they flutter, flap, bob, peck, jerk, jump, hop, and generally move quickly, often spastically, and offer more gamescatship than a mouse with spring-loaded boots and catnip for fur.

We have always had bird feeders where cats can watch but not touch. (I think having a feeding station that attracts birds cats can reach is a dirty trick, a real cheap shot.) We call our no-kill vantage points "cat television." Take a moment if you haven't done so lately, and watch cats watching birds. "Riveted" is nowhere near strong enough a word. They are transfixed, transmuted; their lower jaw quivers; they make anxious little chittering sounds; their intent is the purest of pure evil. And hence a quandary.

There is no way that I know to keep cats from hunting if they are so inclined unless it is to imprison

Mr. Toad at Peace with Himself. Poison glands in his skin make him so sour (or bitter?) to the taste that the cats and dogs leave him alone. He has his own ceramic toad house near the front door, but he uses it only when the sun is high. Most of the time he goes about in his dour way, having at Thistle Hill's ample store of insect life. He is at peace with everyone and doesn't move when man or beast is near. He just stares back.

them. Since that really isn't practicable here, because they always get out, we have to deal with that quandary. Belling a cat is nice, and Victorian in tone, but won't do the nightingale much good.

Birds, unfortunately, as well as small mammals and even reptiles are a cat's *natural* prey. Everything small is game except the majority of amphibians. They have bitter glands in their skin to discourage predators. Our big, fat, jolly toads here at Thistle Hill can hop through a congregation of our cats and not draw a sideways glance. We have a ceramic toad house on the front porch, and cats come and go, passing within inches of it every day. There usually is a fist-sized toad at the front door of the shelter or not far from it. Nary a look! Complete disinterest on the part of the Thistle Hill Regulars. Anything else that size would become a perforated little soccer ball in moments.

Where is the balance of concern to be found? How should we view this matter of life and death? I am a bird watcher, and I know bird-watchers who will kill a cat on sight, yet I do love not only our Regulars but other people's cats and dogs with a passion. The animals they kill are prey species to more than domestic cats. They are prey species period. Snakes, raccoons, foxes, weasels, hawks, owls, skunks, all kinds of animals prey on the small birds and mammals, especially on nestlings and fledglings. That means in order to survive these species have developed a reproductive rate to accommodate the anticipated attrition by predation. Enough are born so many can die. An elephant bears a single young every six to eight years, while in that same period of time a hen codfish (yes, lady codfish are called hens) will lay between 250,000,000 and 350,000,000 eggs! Nature does allow for mortality.

All of this approaches the matter of killing from a game manager's species point of view, however, and is valid only up to a point. But we human beings are a sentimental lot. And I for one am all for that. I don't despise my humanity. I cherish it. What about the one cardinal, the one baby rabbit, the one bluebird? Their species can spare them, but can we? Do we not regard with pity and some sadness the baby anything, bluebird or zebra, when it is killed in a brutal fashion, however natural that may be, just because there are so many more?

I once sat in an open Jeep at a place called Ruhunu on what was then Ceylon, now Sri Lanka, and watched a magnificent leopard stalk and kill a male peacock while he was displaying. I was thrilled to see the great cat at work but profoundly saddened by what his work entailed. I have watched two female lions on the back of a Cape buffalo in Kenya literally tear the poor animal down to the ground. I have watched a mother cheetah teach her young how to hunt by giving them a live baby Thomson's gazelle to practice on. They released and caught it again and again. The cats thrill me, their prey sadden me, but in time you do get to realize emotionally as well as intellectually that that is the way nature works, no less for the animals we have domesticated than for those we haven't and surely never will.

•

BULLETIN FROM THE BARN . . . This just in. Pam Holder sent a message down with Karen. She has not only located the skittery little gray job, but she has it sitting on bales of hay beside her and she can pat it, this over just a few days. This is a cat that will readily turn the corner, obviously. Earlier reports of its asocial nature, like Mark Twain's premature obituary, were grossly exaggerated. Pam's pet cat recently died, and she has asked to take this one home. Of course. A good, caring home is the name of the game. The big gray tabby, a portly puss, is still out there, too. Jean Valjean is in no danger of being crowded, not in that hay and horse hangar, but there is movement out there, a real ebb and flow. It is a living system that may be hard on rats but is great for cats.

•

Although we frequently talk of adding birds to the zoo that is Thistle Hill Farm—peacocks, guinea fowl, and various exotic breeds of ducks, geese, and chickens have been considered and none ruled out—we still have only the two feathered members, the blue-and-yellow macaws, Quito the male and "baby" Bizou Bizou, his future mate.

QUITO was captive bred and not stolen from a rain forest. The theft of wildlife from the wild for the pet trade is a sin! Quito is the original *crunch-bird*. He has a wicked sense of humor and an awesome set of mandibles. He is raucous, bright, and talks like—well, a very, very articulate blue-and-yellow macaw. He also giggles,

*Warning! Interestingly enough, the only warning sign
at Thistle Hill Farm does not have to do with a mighty
steer or half-ton-and-more horses or dogs with mouths
full of teeth or cats with claws. The warning concerns
two beautiful, picturesque birds, captive-bred blue-and-
yellow macaws, that I doubt weigh much more than
five pounds combined. It is indeed better for strangers
not to poke around through the fencing. That is an
invitation to at least gnaw a little.*

guffaws, barks, brays, sneezes, coughs, snorts, whines,
whispers, and says *hello* a hundred times an hour. When
he is in gear he can do a Camille that Garbo never could
have. When he is not saying *hello,* he is reassuring you
by saying *good boy.* He loves to hear himself talk. He only
gets really loud if you pick up the phone, and then he
can break wineglasses. People on the other end of the
phone are often startled, and I find myself stumbling
through absurd explanations, even going as far as mum-
bling something inane about having a terrible cold. He
probably sounds a great deal more intelligent than he
actually is, although his running commentary can be
amazingly appropriate.

BIZOU BIZOU is also a captive-bred blue-and-yellow macaw. She was hatched in Ohio on August 21, 1992, and came to us at about twelve weeks, as sweet as Quito is arrogant. For the first year they are living in separate but large cages (six feet high, thirty-six by thirty-six inches on the sides) four feet apart. In eight months they will go together in a twelve-foot outside cage. It is romantically set under a huge, ancient black walnut tree. When she is between two and three, Bizou Bizou and Quito will almost certainly breed. That should be exciting. We have never waited for eggs to hatch before.

If you have not had experience with the large

macaws, you must understand what they really are—feathered bolt cutters. How a bird that weighs less than three pounds (the feathers are very deceiving) can crack a nut a two-hundred-pound man would have to deal with on an anvil with a hammer is amazing.

We saw an example of that mandible might and have a sadder but wiser dog to prove it. A lot of people think that macaws, members of the parrot family of birds, live on seeds and perhaps the odd raisin now and then. Not so. They eat just about anything people eat including meat. They love a chicken leg as a treat and after the meat and tendons are gone literally pulverize the bone to get at the juices inside. Nothing is left.

One day Quito dropped a chicken bone, and it lay on the bottom of his cage while he worked over some grapes or something else special enough to hold him on a perch instead of going after the bone immediately. Topy the Whippet decided he would like that bone for himself and got one of his paws inside to pull it out. Topy is a great manipulator and can handle most doorknobs if he really wants to. We refer to him affectionately as the "locksmith." On this occasion he would have been better off not testing his skill. Quito descended; Topy went to the hospital—six stitches. He is much less inclined to interact with macaws now.

Each of the cats has had to come to terms with having two birds in the kitchen. For the most part they have acted like Jean Valjean with the cock pheasant, agreeing that the big ones are fun to watch but are better left untouched, particularly since they make such raucous, threatening sounds.

The only exception to this natural and very sensible caution we know of, in fact, is Mary Todd Lincoln, one of the three young cats Teddy is raising. She is the oldest of the three and recently has been allowed hours out of the dungeon each day, mixing easily with the other animals. The macaws were new to her, and before anyone realized what she had done she went from the kitchen floor to a banquette to a shelf by the window to the top of Quito's cage. For some reason Quito took it all in good humor and although Mary Todd Lincoln did get a right smart and, I am sure, smarting South American bite on the butt and more than a little bit of pressure put on her tail, she was lifted down intact and unbloodied. Quito had her cornered up there and could have done real surgery on her, but he was in a forgiving mood. Mary Todd Lincoln won't be looking down on any macaws from the tops of their cages in the near future, I would wager, and she, like the other cats, walks just a little bit faster when she is passing between the two bird cages.

Duncan the Border Collie is even funnier. He must have gotten himself nailed when we didn't know about it. Every time he passes Quito's cage he lifts his lip ever so slightly and gives the softest little secret *grrrr*. It is a kind of mini-snarl, something private between him and Quito.

We do hope to add some barnyard birds eventually

Duncan, the Border Collie, Plays Solo-Soccer—when he has nothing else that requires herding. The cats hate it when he tries to herd them. They have no sense of humor about him or his imperatives.

(we have already been offered a pair of peacocks as a gift), but the cats and the dogs worry me. What about when they have a clutch? Would the cats stalk them? Once we have worked out a safe containment system for the young we'll probably do something and give the Thistle Hill Regulars a new channel to watch on cat television. Duncan will simply have to learn that he can't herd them. Perhaps we should get geese first. They can put any dog or cat in its place. There is no teacher of good manners to match a goose. More than one silly honker sent me shinnying up a tree when I was a kid in rural Massachusetts.

Dogs and cats are an easy match in our homes in part because as competitors they could very often work things out in the wild and make their point without having to slaughter each other every time they were in the same area. No such natural accommodation exists in nature between cats and birds. Birds are prey and any cat large enough to take on the challenge, I am sure, will kill any bird it can get to and overcome. It is more a measure of how far cats have come in the on-going process of domestication to see them with birds than it is to see them with dogs. When a cat tolerates a bird, it really is doing things our way.

The Photographer's Lure Is Irresistible to Marmalade.
But her pose shows her agility and grace to advantage.
Note the tail stuck out for balance, the straight hind
legs, and the length of neck. A nicely conformed critter
she is, by and large. She has nice length of whiskers,
too, and her intensity speaks of intelligence. Marma-
lade, thy name is cat!

12

To Be Considered

A GREAT MANY PEOPLE think of domestication as a finite point, something like home base, rather than a process that probably never will stop in our pets unless we lose interest in the results. It is difficult to imagine that happening, given the degree to which we have been involved with our animal companions up to now. Ever and never are terribly long times, of course, so we will avoid the temptation to say *unconditionally* that it "never" can happen, but I believe we can say it will be another very long time before man will break the hug-a-pet habit.

There is not the faintest hint that we are even looking in the petless direction, much less moving there. In fact, the opposite seems to be true. Increased isolation and alienation in our own society inspires ever more people to seek additional solace and easy companionship. Nonjudgmental friends are the best kind ever in a world of pressure, stress, and *picky-picky-picky.*

It is possible, I suppose, that one day our computers will mean more to us than we can imagine them doing so now, but again, they probably will not transcend the tool/machine/device category for a long, long time. To do that they would have to coerce us into not thinking of them as "its" but as "he/shes." That has been predicted to happen, and if it does we may lose more than our interest in our pets. We may see our own reproductive rate drop below the species-sustaining level. That would be the final seduction of man by his own toys. There is not much future for a species that takes a Nintendo game on a honeymoon. That would be the ultimate "farewell to arms."

Personally, I don't anticipate that fatal mechanization of human emotions happening. It would be my guess, and I don't think I am being Pollyannaish, that we will be liking each other in a special way and our pets, too, for some time to come. (The two imperatives apparently arise in the same corner of our very complex minds.)

As long as we do want our pets, rejoice in our pets, need our pets actually, their evolution is guaranteed to continue as a biological inevitability as well as a natural outgrowth of the continuing process of domestication. I don't think the process of evolution is ever really finished, not with the higher animals, at least. I suspect that in the really complicated animals like cats, the end of evolution would be the extinction of the species.

If we lost interest in cats they would very quickly, as these things go, evolve away from their present domesticated form and possibly emerge as some kind of genetic monstrosity for our having meddled and then walked away from our own creation. Given the dynamics of living, I believe running full speed is just about staying in place. I doubt that evolution even has the potential for completion built into it. Like space exploration, evolution is an open-ended adventure, certainly within any time frame we can deal with. By definition it could not have a deadline or completion date. It isn't carpentry; it is the nearest thing we know to magic. Anyone who says they don't believe in miracles has never really thought very much about evolution. It just keeps on getting better and better with each new good idea opening up the potential for heaven alone knows how many more. If it goes awry, with things getting worse and worse, the outcome is inevitable and a species becomes a fossil, first a living one, then a real one for future generations of intelligent creatures to discover. Either way there is a door beyond the door beyond the door, probably ad infinitum.

If we are to allow for the "in progress" status of both evolution and domestication of both form (morphology) and behavior (ethology) of our animal companions (and how could we not?) we have to establish some perspective to understand the Thistle Hill Regulars or any other cats, for that matter, yours included.

As suggested earlier, there is an enormous time difference in the history of domestication of dogs and cats. Dog genes probably have been under our thumb five times as long as those of the feline kind. And that really is what it has been all about, control. The name of the game has been and still is now, design-an-animal. There has been a tremendous amount of our own ego

Lucia. Found on Madison Avenue in Manhattan on the eve of a major blizzard, Lucia the Italian Greyhound came to us unspayed and with a large mammary tumor. Surgery corrected both conditions, and she settled in like a tiny contessa full of demands. She obviously had not lived with cats and still is afraid to get really close with them. With other dogs she is bossy and superior in her attitude. Her diet is almost impossible to believe; she loves cat food, moist and dry, all salad vegetables, melon, anchovies, cheese, of course, squash of all kinds, any kind of pasta with any kind of sauce, eggplant, anything, in fact, except dog food. Some of our cats outweigh her.

involved, but of course we refer to that as aesthetics. After all, God created man in *his* own image. Where could we have picked up a different role model? We have recreated our pets over and over again, following idealized images of beauty. Very often we have shown little or no regard for any function beyond our own pleasure. Is a Persian cat, magnificent as it can be to look at and stroke, a functional design from the cat's point of view? And its canine counterparts, Shih Tzu and Lhasa Apso, Affenpinscher and Italian Greyhound, are they really functional?

If any animal was domesticated earlier than the dog it would have been the goat, but that is only a maybe; archaeologists tell us that maybe the dog wasn't first. Despite their very long time in our care, dogs still display many wolf characteristics. Xyerius, our incredible, big, mostly white Greyhound, frequently smiles by rolling back his upper lip and showing his teeth. There is absolutely no threat in that, although more than one postperson and UPS person has leaped back into their vehicle when Xyerius has greeted them in the driveway. The sequence or event is not even remotely akin to a dog's snarl. It is just a slightly askew genetic signal from Xyerius's ancestors to say: *"I submit. You, good sir or madam, are alpha, and the beta role is just fine with me."* Here the poor dear is telling new people on his own home turf not only that they are welcome, but that he won't challenge their superiority as human beings, and they're diving through their truck windows, screaming, *"Call off your dog! Call off your dog!"* They can't believe Xyerius is acting like a dog-come-of-wolf and not like another human being.

If Xyerius is still getting signals, however on or off the mark they may be, after a hundred and fifty centuries of our caring for his genes, what are our cats listening to after only forty centuries? The call of the wild must still be loud indeed for our feline newcomers. It must be a deafening roar demanding that they disobey us, break their covenant with an artificial force, us, that would dare diddle about with their genes. Any accommodation that cats show our way of life can't come easily. We should give them their due, at least a kind of "A" for effort.

We are, by the way, able to fix an approximate date for the cat's domestication more readily than we are for the dog's, because records from dynastic Egypt are rather better than they are from the cave. Man was still well back in the bosom of the Stone Age, in our pre-agriculture phase, when the dog came on board the Ark, but well this side of it when the cat was invited in from the cold. The use of the word *ark* actually is an interesting image. I sometimes think that is what Thistle Hill Farm is evolving into.

The behavior of an animal (including our own kind) is apparently an ill-defined mix of genetic signals, such as the one Xyerius uses to scare the wits out of people, combined in some way with individually learned behavior (from events in a single animal's own history) and an unknown number of variables, such as opportunity, chance, and geography.

The puma (aka cougar, mountain lion, panther, painter, red lion, American lion, and scores of other names, at least, in English, French, Spanish, and Portuguese, not to begin to include names in aboriginal tongues) has had the greatest north-south range of any cat species in modern times. The species has ranged from southern Canada to southern Argentina in my life span. That has had them on the pampas, in mountains, in snow, in swamps like those attending the Everglades, in burning deserts, in semi-arid montane and lowland zones, in foothills, in rain forests and jungles like those hard by the Amazon, on the plains of the American West and in boreal forests, along the coast of both the

Atlantic and the Pacific oceans and far, far inland. We have to think, I believe, that that enormous spread in habitat opportunities contributes to many different cats, albeit of one species, just as learned behavior has and the peculiar puma genes have. For whatever other factors play a role in its behavior, a species is at least partially a prisoner of its inherited characteristics, survival skills, and reproductive mandates. In an animal as immensely complicated as a cat, wild or domestic, you start with that package, the genes, and then add behavior directly learned by the individual, and many unknown factors such as geographic opportunities. It is an amazing blend that simply is not decipherable. I purposely do not say *not now decipherable* or *not decipherable yet* because I am not at all convinced that it ever will be. (Again allowing for the fact that "ever" is a terribly long time and one not easily defined or addressed.)

What is the difference between habitat opportunities—isn't that about learned behavior?—and the kind of learning required to respond to the almost inevitably disruptive proximity of man, for example? Good question. I am glad I asked it. Actually, the two are close. Where they differ, I believe, is in the dynamics of change. Two pumas of the same species, in this case *Felis concolor,* one living in the Everglades and one in the mountains of Utah, learn over a long period of time how to avoid local pitfalls (you can fall a lot further in Utah than you can in Florida, where maximum elevation above sea level in the 'Glades is ten feet) and make the most out of opportunities. The species and therefore the behavior of venomous snakes differ. Different kinds of cover are available and different kinds of food and therefore competition. That is one kind of learning peculiar to geographical races or varieties of the same species.

Then there is the even more dynamic kind of learning: man moves in and starts ranching or mining; deforestation is launched; prey species are driven off; swamps are drained; rivers are diverted. Those phenomena may happen over a fairly wide area, hundreds of square miles, yet affect only a few individual cats. That gives limited opportunity for some few cats to learn new accommodations during their tutorial period with their mother.

The significant point is we don't *know* the relative importance of learned (on any level) and genetic information. We are not even close. A lot of doctoral candidates are going to have to spend an enormous amount of time clocking a great many white rats running around in a lot of mazes before even the beginning of an answer is in view. B. F. Skinner, the late professor of psychology at Harvard, thought that environmental influence was minuscule when compared to the inherited package, but a lot of people disagree with that view. I have the temerity to think him not right. I even told him so back in 1966. He looked at me benignly, with pity in his eyes. But we don't really know relative values here, not by any means. One has to wonder if it is even knowable, at least in any time frame with which we can deal. Perhaps not.

What all that means is that your cat and mine represent an unknown mix of mysterious exterior influ-

Martha Custis Washington High in a Black Walnut Tree. The huge black walnut trees offer wonderful horizontal perches, fine rough bark that must be a joy to climb, and plenty of shade. The cats love this one. It is a patriarch seventy feet across the drip line, over a hundred feet tall. I should imagine that by the time a cat has explored all of Thistle Hill Farm, all the high branches and hidden crannies in and out of the buildings, he would be quite well along in years. Our cats never stop their exploring, not unless the weather really is intolerable.

ences and interior elements. Their personalities come from that blend and so do their destinies, whatever they may be. It would be enormously useful to understand that blend better than we do in designing our relationship with such close companions. But that is not to be, not now. We both have to feel our ways into any love affair we enter with each other. After all, really, how much intellectualizing do you have to engage in to love a cat, or to celebrate the fact that a cat loves you? At Thistle Hill Farm we just do what comes naturally. That is the hedonistic, existential approach. Hey, if it feels good, go for it! That's the way cats "think."

Traits and factors that we feel we need to alter do

arise in the genes of an animal. Surely we will attempt to do so, for it is utter nonsense to think that we have stopped meddling or will stop in the foreseeable future. The kind of genetic manipulation that we have been into since before we had an inkling that anything like genes even existed must naturally lead in our time to bioengineering. That is as much a part of our own evolution as of the evolution of the animals we control in such a profound way. If the traits that we feel the need to alter are genetic, then we may elect to deal with them the way we have through the domestication process thus far, by selective breeding, or carry it all forward to that next giant step.

We are already chopping genes up routinely, using enzymes for scalpels. That is going to become more and more common, and I pray we will continue to use the restraint we apparently have used so far although much of that work is still being done behind closed doors. If I am wrong about restraint, a house cat that weighed ninety pounds, walked on its hind legs, and smoked cigars would not be a pretty picture.

If, on the other hand, the behavioral trait that concerns us is one that is learned by an individual animal or by a small population from regional opportunities, then our approach should be behavior modification rather than genetic alteration by breeding or engineering.

We can isolate and analyze individual traits, we think—some, not many,—and deal with them, but the whole beast still eludes us. Perhaps that is what people mean when they say cats are mysterious. We don't know what they are made of except in the most general terms. And wouldn't it be wonderful to know? Wouldn't it be grand to know where this may all lead, what the potential really is of the cat's magic genes?

Scan the breed books and see how very much more elastic canine genes seem to be than their feline counterparts. The largest domestic cat in the world (except, perhaps, for some outrageous freak) probably doesn't weigh much more than eight times as much as the smallest. The largest breeds of dogs, on the other hand, routinely weigh eighty times as much as the smallest of the toy breeds.

There is, however, another way of viewing cats. Ranging across the entire feline family, not just a single species, the cats very greatly in size and habits. A really large Siberian or Amur tiger is a staggering size. It can weigh almost eight hundred pounds, while one of the lesser cats, like our domestic cats' North African ancestor, will weigh in at a relatively few pounds. What if that family-wide feline elasticity should eventually prove to be reflected in the one species, *Felis familiaris,* the domestic cat?

There is nowhere near the range in size among the wild canines that there is among the wild felines. The largest wild canine is the wolf and it usually doesn't weigh even a hundred pounds. Our smallest domestic dog is about one thirty-second the weight of the wolf and our largest dog over twice the size. With our cat we might be about to uncork a very exciting bottle. The best of the cat surely is yet to come. Who knows what the Regulars might look like—or behave like—a thousand years from now, or a few dozen years in the future if bioengineering really does start to figure in the mix?

I went to work for the MSPCA in Methuen, Massachusetts, for ten cents an hour fifty-five years ago and watched in stunned amazement as dogs and cats were put to death by the hundreds. In those days the filthy, gagging exhaust fumes from an old truck were used, an unroadworthy old clunker kept for just that one dreadful assignment. The exhaust was piped through a nasty old piece of hosing into a glass-topped, coffinlike container that was stuffed with terrified animals at least once a day.

The slaughter went on five days a week and it saddened me terribly. It didn't do any good not to look, to be somewhere else on the farm when it was PTS ("put to sleep") time. I could hear that truck—I still can when I think about it—and I knew. I frequently cried myself to sleep at night and then only to have ghastly nightmares. More than that, it stunned me. I couldn't stop thinking about it. I couldn't understand how such things could possibly be necessary. I don't think any ten-year-old could.

Today, as the president of the ASPCA headquartered in New York, the largest hands-on humane organization in the world, I understand somewhat, but I find the truth not one bit less shattering. It is an awful truth and it tells a lot more about us than it does about the animals we kill through our moral bankruptcy.

Time and again in this book I have tried to stress how necessary it is for us to spay and neuter our pets except in cases where their genetic material is truly needed to keep breeds from becoming extinct. A moratorium on all breeding is not the answer, because the breeds of cats and dogs—and purebred animals are just as precious as random-bred—those purebreds will become extinct in a very few years if they are not cherished and maintained. They are cultural artifacts, agreed-upon standards of perfection, and if we lose them we will lose a part of our own history, a part of ourselves.

While it is not cruel to individual animals to allow a species to become extinct, it is cruel to history past and future. It is total disregard for tradition. It is incredible cosmic vandalism.

It is true that if an animal is not born it can never be abused, abandoned, or put to death in a shelter because there is no home for it. It is difficult to imagine that somewhere between ten and twenty million cats and dogs are put to sleep every year. Where do they come from? How does such a horror come to be?

Most of the animals killed in shelters are not puppies and kittens, they are dogs and cats. They range in age from recently matured to very old. Why do they end up in such desperate straits? Indifference in a plastic throwaway society, mostly. Bad animal management, without the obedience training necessary in the vast majority of cases, is a big factor and so are aggressive tendencies, overlooked until they become overt aggression. Fear biting. Preventable disease. Lack of control of urban and suburban animals. Overproduction. Whim purchases and adoptions. But all of those factors are but species of indifference.

•

BULLETIN FROM THE BARN . . . I should explain why I am relying on bulletins instead of watching the cats myself, as I have for most of the material for this book. In the middle of transcribing my notes on the Regulars into book form, I had a nasty fall here at the farm. (Cats are not the only species subject to misadventure!) I broke my hip and for a month and a half, while waiting for a replacement to join my skeleton, during which time the bulletins are being accepted, I have

Martha Custis Washington Loves Camping. There is a fully equipped safari tent down at the edge of the marsh, so if anyone wants to wake up closer to nature than even an old farmhouse allows, the tent is waiting. It is one of Martha's favorite places on the farm. It is the first place to look for her if she is missing. When the tent is used, she loves it. She is a real safari cat.

been confined to a wheelchair on the upper floor of the house. It is temporary, and I will soon be on crutches for a week or two and then a cane. But getting to the barn now is totally out of the question. Climbing up on top of the bales of hay to sit and wait for the cats to appear is even more hopeless. Anyway, here is the latest report and it is something of a mystery, or at least it contributes to one. The new cat, the dark tabby, is a bobtail.

Martha Custis Washington, brought here by Karen from the nearby Pennsylvania countryside, is a bobtail. One of the cats that showed up at the Gentrys' across the way not long ago was a bobtail. Daughter Pamela and her husband, Joe, have just taken in a waif they call Noelle. That is about twelve minutes from here unless you are a crow; then it is much less. Noelle is a bobtail. I don't know what percentage of the domestic cats in the world are bobtails or how assertive the gene is that calls for that style of cat, but we are seeing a surprising number of them around here. Is there a prepotent old tom carrying that gene working through here imprinting himself via unspayed, uncared-for queens? Something like that must be the case. Further, Martha Custis Washington and Noelle and reportedly the new tabby in the barn all are higher and heavier in the rear than rather more ordinary cats. Manx? Who can say?

•

There are two problems we have seen here at Thistle Hill that virtually all multiple cat owners see sooner or later, whether their cats have been in residence one at a time or in herds and bunches. Both problems contribute immeasurably to the unhappy fate of far too many cats that are sooner or later deemed unadoptable. Unfortunately some people are so assertive, so positive on these subjects, that it can be difficult for not terribly experienced cat owners to get a fix on the problems and know what they should do. I don't have *the* answer, but I do have ours.

I have walked down the aisles between the cages in shelters all over America for decades and seen cage after cage with a red sign that says: SCRATCHES FURNITURE. Sometimes there isn't a separate sign, but the damning information is on the history card attached to the cage door as the reason for the surrender or turn-in. Why make an issue of it? Why even mention it? Because it is unfair to well-intentioned new owners and certainly unfair to the poor, powerless cats to adopt them out under false pretenses. It is more than unfair. It is cruel. The cat will just come back, if it is lucky, or be otherwise disposed of. "Otherwise" can be the harshest punishment of all, the unknown. A cat that gets passed around or adopted again and again would literally be better off being put to sleep. Eventually, after it has been made hopelessly neurotic, it probably will be.

What, then, do you do with a cat that tears your drapes and curtains and shreds your carpeting, slip covers, and upholstery? In a few hours a "scratcher" can do hundreds or even thousands of dollars' worth of damage. A great many people faced with really bad damage give up without trying because they feel let down, betrayed, scorned when they have tried to be kind and accepting. That's how a great many cats end up on death row.

Most cats that try their paws at destroying your home can be turned around quite easily. They are not "sharpening their claws" as is so often claimed. They are shedding the old sheaths on their claws, stripping them off to make places for new ones. It is reflexive behavior, not intentional vandalism at all. It is most often done just after a cat wakes up from a nap. Wild species use trees, standing and fallen, the rougher the bark the better. The ritual is performed in company with a stretching and pulling exercise. It is not done in spite or anger or to get revenge, as is so often stated. If we love our cats as much as we say we do, then we can give them the dignity of remaining cats and not have negative human behavior and thought processes attributed to them. A cat surely does not have cognitive powers sophisticated enough to deal with anything like revenge. Nasty people seek revenge. Cats are not now nor have they ever been nasty people. As for the scratching cat? Boredom? Possibly. Reflex? Almost certainly. Playfulness? Probably. Revenge? Certainly not!

What can you do with a furniture scratcher besides getting rid of it? The directions are in every how-to cat book and there are a whole flock of them in stores and libraries. Supply both horizontal and vertical scratching posts. You can make them yourself out of scrap carpeting and wood, or you can buy them made up and ready to plunk down and entice your cat. Some are regular jungle gyms, some are baited with catnip, and most seem to work. Some have slanting surfaces as well, and that does give your cat all of the options. One scratching station should be kept near where your cat naps—and that is usually a pretty routine matter—and be waiting for him when he wakes up.

What if a cat simply will not be weaned away from furniture, and the repair bills continue to mount? If it is really hopeless is there anything else to be done besides getting rid of a friend? Your veterinarian can get you shields to glue on your cat's claws but most people won't go to the "trouble," strangely enough. That brings us to the most controversial of all aspects of cat owning —declawing. There is more hysteria surrounding that one word than any other single word in the cat owner's vocabulary.

There are more self-proclaimed, world-class experts on the subject of declawing than on almost any other I know. Actually, for a humane organization, given the humane crises we face every day—cats being stolen by the thousands and being embalmed for schoolchildren to dissect, some before they are dead; cats being stolen by the thousands and used as live bait for pit bulls to tear apart in training exercises; pets being stolen for illegal sale to questionable laboratories; cats being used for food by some Asian immigrants; cats used for ritual sacrifice; and a score more—on a scale of one to ten, declawing is a two or at the worst a three.

Declawing is not ripping the cat's claws out with a pair of rusty pliers. It is a surgical procedure just as spaying and neutering are.

Declawing is done under general anesthesia. There could be no excuse for its not being done that way.

By no stretch of the imagination, however, is declawing a routine procedure like spaying and neutering, and it must never be considered as such. There is nothing natural or routine about it. It is a form of mutilation.

Without doubt declawing entails a period of postoperative pain. So does an appendectomy. So does spaying, which involves opening the abdomen. So does neutering, which involves opening the scrotal sac. So does circumcision, which in infants is done without anesthesia. Surgery of any kind almost always involves postoperative discomfort to varying degrees.

Declawed cats can still defend themselves. In declawing only the front feet are done, and other animals do not know the cats have had surgery. Cats in great danger don't use their front claws. They roll over on their backs and rake with their hind claws, which are left untouched. Declawed cats still climb trees albeit probably not as well as cats who are intact, or quite as fast. The cats themselves forget about the procedure because as long as they live they continue to go through the stretching/scratching routine even though there are no claws to desheath.

After about a week to ten days postsurgery declawed cats can return to using their regular litter box. Average postoperative hospital stay for declawed cats is twenty-four to thirty-six hours.

Do we declaw the cats at Thistle Hill Farm? Very, very rarely. In fact we have had only one cat declawed since we moved down here. In East Hampton we found it essential on a few very rare occasions. Who is declawed here? Only Teddy. Not because of furniture, but because of the ferocious way he attacked every animal he encountered before Emmy and then his three adopted children. We were afraid he would blind or otherwise maim other animals, and with small grandchildren and house guests it is inevitable that doors get left ajar. Curious cats and dogs do want to see the Man in the Iron Mask for themselves. After all, they could smell him, so they knew he was there. Teddy was dangerous (certainly not to people) and had to be disarmed as a humanitarian act to other animals.

When is declawing justified if the dollars and cents of slipcovers and not animals' lives are at stake? *Only,* in my estimation, when the cat really cannot be weaned away from furniture and drapes, when nothing else works and everything has been tried, and when it really has come down to a choice between declawing or euthanasia. When it does come down to whether an animal loses its claws or its life, I opt for sustaining life. The important point is that the choice is not academic. Every year unknown scores of thousands of cats are killed because they are identified as furniture wreckers, the kiss of death, and no one will give them a home.

In summary, at Thistle Hill Farm we do not generally declaw our cats; in fact, we very rarely do. Normally, we would only do it if the cat could not otherwise be kept as a house pet. We would not take an indoor-outdoor cat and consign it to the barn if it turned out to be a furniture destroyer. That, I think, would be cruel and unusual punishment.

Thinking as we do, have we sustained any damage

Emmy in the Birdbath. Emmy likes the birdbath so much for sunning herself that we leave it dry most of the time. There are plenty of other places for the birds to wet themselves down. The stainless-steel porpoises are content no matter what the conditions and in the winter look rather nice with snowy caps. Emmy, it is plain to see, is a thinker. Her affair with Teddy was long since over when this picture was taken. They ignore each other.

from cats clawing furniture? None that we weren't willing to sustain. None that we didn't think worth tolerating and repairing until we could get the culprit turned around.

Still, declawing is not a four-letter word; neither should it engender hysteria, white heat, or blind rage. Our pets ask of us that we be sensible, reasonable, and rational in the management of their affairs. An emotional tantrum is none of the above, particularly when matters at hand have not been considered from all angles and all options and their consequences evaluated.

The worst of all cat-in-the-family problems, in our estimation, occurs when a cat suddenly decides that the litter box is history. Any cat may suddenly make this least of all desirable switches, although happily most do not.

One of the most attractive characteristics of the cat as a pet is its fabled cleanliness. Cats are naturally clean, about themselves, about their young, and about their toilet. They don't have to be walked, and in by far most homes they do not have to go outside at all. That is one of the reasons that cats have now overtaken dogs and are the number-one pet in America. It is estimated that there are sixty million cats in American homes, fifty-five million dogs. The litter box instead of the walk in the snow or rain or freezing cold on dangerous American city streets late at night surely is a factor. You are unlikely to get mugged while changing your cat's litter pan.

That expectation of cleanliness makes it difficult for people to accept a cat's fall from grace. It is usually taken as a personal affront when it occurs. Again, owners feel betrayed, and in a sense they have been. It usually is unexpected, inexplicable, and very smelly. It can be a difficult problem to reverse permanently, and I personally believe it is a prime cause of cat surrenders and abandonments. A great many cats "from very good homes" get put down by private veterinarians every year because the vets and their clients have been unable to solve the problem. A great many veterinarians routinely recommend it as the best way out of a nasty situation.

There is no easy answer and certainly no sure solution. There is no way of making your cat understand that it is, in so many cases, committing suicide. Most people can tolerate a certain amount of inappropriate behavior on the part of their pets, but find this one intolerable because it can't be kept a secret. In short order, despite the owner's best efforts, the house begins to reek. "Cat odor" is terribly offensive and is pervasive to the point where I have known people who were wrestling with the problem who would not invite people into their home. They finally gave up and the poor, misguided cat took a one-way trip to the veterinarian.

If your cat does suddenly start messing or spraying, at least consider the steps we have taken here when it has happened:

1. Have the offender examined by your veterinarian. There can be physical problems, and the first step is to rule them out. Cats are subject to urinary disorders,

Huxley, the Baby Alpaca, Has a Very Sweet Face and a Pleasing Disposition. He is keenly interested in cats and they in him since none of them has traveled in South America, as far as we know.

and if that is what is causing the unwanted behavior you may be able to put an end to it with medication. Even altered males may spray. Neutering goes a long way toward preventing it, but it isn't foolproof. Not many things in life are.

2. Make sure the litter box has been kept clean and its location has not been changed. Is it as accessible as it has always been? Has anything in the way of furniture been added that could worry a cat, something like

stereo speakers or an air conditioner? Have you changed the brand of litter you were using? If so, go back to the old one. In some things cats show a low tolerance for change. But if you are still using the old litter try a new one—and another if that doesn't work. Heaven help us, cats can be fussy.

3. Try using more than one box. Place them strategically, one wherever an accident has occurred. Try to outguess your friend. You are a member of the species presumed to be the more intelligent. Look on that as a challenge. We do with all our pets. Sometimes we even are.

4. Deodorize any room and specifically any area that has been soiled. Don't leave scented invitations for your friend to sin again. There are very good carpet deodorizers now available in your local market and generally in your veterinarian's office, and your hardware store probably rents heavy-duty steam and chemical carpet cleaners. Carpet-cleaning services are not all that expensive and do a good deep-cleaning job. Then deodorize again. Erase all signs of your friend's criminal history.

5. Needless to say, don't stick anybody's nose into anything. Your pet's nose is not the offending part. And cats respond to punishment like ducks do to sand dunes. You will only make your cat uptight, and that is what may be wrong already. Stay cool. Shrieking—at the cat, at your spouse, at the kids, or in the mirror—won't help.

6. If the mistakes have been made in one room

only, try to close that room to pet traffic. Don't allow the felon back to the scene of his crime. This can be a very important step.

7. If the mistakes have been made at a certain time —after you have gone to bed, when you are out, after feeding, when the dog comes in—try to identify that time and prepare for it. Set up a fair-sized crate—an airline shipping crate will do, one designed for a giant dog—and put a fastidiously maintained litter box, a bed, a water bowl, and a little bowl of treats in it and confine your irksome friend at that time. Overnight is fine. All he is supposed to do is sleep then, anyway. I have known this to work very well and then the crate can be dispensed with.

8. Have there been changes in your routine that could lead to resistance? Have you added animals? Have favorite (to the cat) people moved away? In what way(s) has your household changed? Look for causes of stress, and although they may not be repairable it may be possible to relieve some of the pressure your cat is feeling. Then again, it may not; i.e. if your daughter has gotten married and you think that is it, asking the kids to get an annulment would be considered by some as overdoing it. I know of a case where that is exactly what happened. They found a solution that was far better than euthanasia. They all loved the cat anyway. It went to live with the daughter with whom it had slept every night before she left home. The core family adopted another lovely cat from the shelter, which they came to adore, the daughter was happy, now that she had it all,

the son-in-law eventually found out that he had been a closet cat lover all along, and the cat, of course, was delighted. It was as clean as clean can be. She had made her point and survived. For the cat it is a high-risk adventure in trans-species communication.

9. If you have exhausted medical explanations and devices, if your veterinarian is at the shrugging stage, and you can't identify or ameliorate causes of stress or provide your cat with alternatives it will accept, then your options are narrowing rapidly. Go back to suggestion 7 above. Restricting your cat may be your only available choice. After that, it is very hard decision time. What can you live with, and when is enough enough? Only you know the answers to those questions. I know a prominent family going through it even as I write. The whole family is in an uproar, riddled with guilt and doubts. It is one of those problems that is best resolved as quickly as possible once it really has been determined that no solution exists.

10. One option is not open to you. The problem cat is yours and you have to provide the solution. Neither a biting dog nor a cat that either scratches furniture or won't use a litter box can be passed along to the unsuspecting. If you have known and loved the animal, and you won't put up with it, you can pretty well predict that strangers will show even less tolerance when they learn the awful truth. It is a nasty position to be confronted with. With sixty million pet cats in this country, the problem is not a rare one nor is it ever easy to face. To be perfectly candid, I have known far more

failures than success stories. That does not mean that it is not worthwhile to try. You never know. Your cat turned it on, perhaps it will be willing and able to turn it off.

At Thistle Hill Farm we have one and a half pure-bred cats. Alice, of course, is pure Siamese and a very handsome little animal she is, too. The dark, mature Seal-Point Siamese is a kind of symbol of pure breeding and the breed is probably known to more people than any other single breed or style of cat. Teddy appears to be cut from the same cloth, but with shears neither as sharp nor as sure. There could be something else mixed in there, too. He is about as elegant as a concert grand piano with two legs, or an ostrich with one.

We did have Maridadi and her son, Siafu. They were as pure as pure can be—American Shorthair Silver Ash tabbies. Phyllis Barclay, my indwelling mother-in-law and news anchor, has had a couple of regal Persians in her time with us (one black and one champagne), and we have had seven other Siamese cats over the span of thirty-eight years, only two of which were not rescues. We adopted Harriet from a rescue group when she was seventeen. No one else would have her and her owner had just died. And that is it. All of our other cats have been random bred, friends you could look at and say, "Thy name is cat."

Allow me to hold forth, for a moment, on seman-tics. Typically, we refer to mixed-breed animals (this is admittedly more often true of dogs than cats) as mutts, mongrels, and by other regional expressions the disdain of which is often emphasized with the words "only" or "just" preceding them. The whole feeling is of "lesser cat." That lack of image can lead to a lack of concern.

I am holding out for the term "random bred" as the perfectly natural counterpoint to "purebred." It gives our friends with whiskers the dignity they deserve and the kind of identity they need. Please cooperate. In our world today logo is what it is all about, logo and image. With our television-commercial mentality, a breed or nonbreed designation is nothing more or less than a brand name. Would you buy anything as classless as Mutt Soup or Mongrel Denture Glue? How about Preparation H-For-Half-Breed? In contrast, Random Bred has a free, wind-in-the-hair feeling about it. It sounds good enough to be a soap scented with mountain laurel from Ireland in the springtime.

Categorically, random-bred cats need and certainly deserve exactly the same care and consideration, the same nutrition and the same protection against disease that purebred cats require. The idea that they are tougher and less needy is one of the most cruel hoaxes traditional knowledge has played on our cats. It is as dumb as that idea we discussed earlier of its being okay to hurl cats off rooftops because they will be sure to land on their feet. We are dealing with sensitive living creatures, and anything that minimizes their really simple needs is contrary to their well-being. At Thistle Hill Farm it would be unthinkable to separate the Regulars into social strata. (It is bad enough that is done with

people.) The barn cats here eat the same food as the house cats and get the same medical protection against disease and reproduction. Cats constitute a classless society except insofar as they stratify themselves. We should be above that sort of thing.

All our domestic cats come from the same genetic

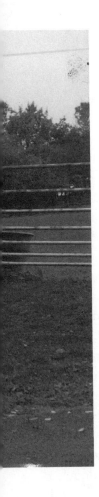

The Chute with Duncan on Patrol—as he almost always is. Huxley is on the left. Both animals respect the fact that this is an electric fence. Everybody touches it once—but seldom twice.

fountain. With purebreds the breeding has been more selective, nothing more arcane than that. It has gone on long enough in the pure breeds with enough line breeding and inbreeding so that the animals now "breed true," replicate themselves. It can reasonably be anticipated that if you breed a purebred Siamese cat with another Siamese cat of equally spotless lineage the litter will be made up of one hundred percent pure Siamese kittens. Once, what was to become the ancestor of the Siamese cat was random bred. It has, however, been refined generation by generation by selecting mates exhibiting characteristics deemed desirable by the aesthetics of the time. A breed of purebred pet, like a piece of music or a work of literature, will be kept alive if it has enduring quality whose aesthetic values cross time boundaries and cultural lines. In every sense a cat like the Siamese and the Persian is a "classic," every bit as much as Mozart's Piano Concerto No. 27 or Shakespeare's *Hamlet,* to be very obvious, are classics.

Every cat that exists in our homes (and every unfortunate that is without a home) is descended from that same source, the North African wildcat. Kittens were stolen from wild stock by the Egyptians and socialized, and after hundreds of generations (of cats, not people) of selective breeding they began to produce kittens that were predictably more like some ideal, then held, of what a cat should be like than they were like their wild ancestors. Somewhere along the line of that continuum the cat could be said to have been domesticated. That means, simply, its genes were under outside control. They had been selectively bred from one form of cat into another that would eventually be celebrated by science with a different species name. Before they were genetically under control, however, when they were just tame or socialized wildcats they were not domesticated.

Egyptian art that has come down to us depicts a cat that barely resembles the ancestral form. The cat that we see (semideified as the goddess Basht or Bastet by the time it was sculpted and painted on papyrus) is slender and elegant, smooth, sleek, and aristocratic. The North African wildcat is cobby, close-coupled (short), low, rather flat-headed, a chunky little roughneck out to kill anything from snakes and rodents to geese and ducks. It is also built to fight over mates and territory and to keep itself from being eaten by everything from crocodiles to hyena. It is anything but elegant and regal. It is a tough survivor in a tough world. Its spirit, if not its inelegant form, has lived on inside our pet cats today, four thousand years removed, visible to us only as behavior.

There are nowhere near as many recognized breeds of cats as there are of dogs. Worldwide (we do not recognize nearly as many breeds in the United States as an international roster would show) there are *perhaps* sixty kinds of purebred cats and almost four hundred and fifty breeds of dogs. The list of breeds currently recognized in the United States follows as an appendix.

What is the right cat for you? No one can know that but you, for the decision is both ethical and aesthetic. Ethically you should hie yourself down to an animal rescue shelter or "pound" and adopt a nice cat-cat before the harried people there have to kill it to make room for others coming through the front door. Don't think kitten so much as the cat the kitten will become or already has become. Kittenhood is a brief episode in the life of a cat, although heaven knows that is a wonderful period of a few months. When you select a mature cat, however, you are choosing a less adoptable animal than a kitten would be and you are more certain of actually saving a life.

Most important, if you already have a cat or two at home, do not take any adopted cat directly there, but plan things so your veterinarian will be on duty. Unless the shelter can give you an up-to-date feline leukemia test report and a record of immunization, including a rabies certificate, these are things you will have to see to yourself. Get your cat or kitten checked out for parasites and ear problems and given a general going-over. Until your veterinarian says it is clear to introduce your new friend to old ones, you are going to have to have isolation—somehow at home or at the veterinarian's hospital for a day or two. Here at Thistle Hill Farm we have an isolation facility in the kennels since airborne diseases are not transmitted between dogs and cats except, theoretically, under extremely rare circumstances, rabies. The way we are set up at the kennels that wouldn't happen even in a worse-case scenario.

I have only bought three cats in my life. There was that first super Siamese, Thai Lin, from a breeder in New York; the second Siamese, Abigail, from a breeder outside of London; and Maridadi, the Silver Ash Tabby, from a judge and breeder in New Jersey. I am, therefore, not exactly an expert in buying a cat, but I do know that you will pay far less, know more about what you are getting, and have a better assurance if not guarantee of health and quality if you go directly to an experienced breeder.

In the appendices are the addresses for the major cat registries. Check with them for breeders' names if you are already absolutely certain of the breed you want. If there is any question in your mind, get a list of cat shows sanctioned by the registries and go to one or two all-breed events. At least you'll find out if you are allergic to cats.

Enjoy yourself. Wear comfortable shoes. Walk the aisles, see the cats, talk to the experts, breeders and judges, and then get your name on the list for a kitten of your chosen breed with a breeder you feel you can trust.

Don't try to figure out what is going on with the judging. Just ignore it. If you ask anyone they will just lie to you to impress you that they are "in." In fact, they are likely to be as confused as you are. The trick is to stand there and look knowing. It isn't difficult. If anyone asks your opinion of anything just say, *"Tough choice, really tough,"* On the word *"really"* try thrusting your lower jaw forward.

If you are treated rudely or otherwise badly handled, relax; you can handle that. After all, you are trying to "take a kitten away" from the person you are attempting to deal with. The fact that you have your checkbook in your hand for all to see is not part of the equation. There is the breeder whose love and hard work, perhaps over a period of many years, produced the little wonder; there is the little wonder itself all cuddly and helpless; and then there is an interloper, you, trying to disrupt things with talk of money. You are a threat. Be tolerant. After all, you either are or are about to become a cat owner, too. Then you can be as crazy as the rest of us. It doesn't take long.

As for the Thistle Hill Regulars, we don't buy cats, we certainly don't breed cats, we just take life as it

The Tennis Net Path from Grass to Grass. The hoofed animals of Thistle Hill Farm are rotated through five pastures to keep the grass growing. So they can move across the driveway without running out, two tennis nets are stretched across, forming the transit lane. Before this innovation was put in place, we used to have the most hysterical Wild West roundups. Humboldt is a very well behaved animal, but still he might take it into his mind to explore and thereby get into trouble. The tennis nets are safety nets.

comes along and it certainly does. We like things to be tranquil, as tranquil as things can be when you add thirty-two miscellaneous animal lives to an already dynamic human family. I guess "ark" would apply. We are one big happy ark and we couldn't care less what other people say.

Cat Registries

There are a number of registering bodies in the United States and abroad. Cat shows are generally staged under the auspices of one of them. They publish the breed standards and show rules for the shows they sanction.

In the United Kingdom there is one registry:

GOVERNING COUNCIL OF THE CAT FANCY
    4–6 Penel Orlieu
    Bridgwater, Somerset
    TA6 3PG
    ENGLAND

In the United States there are quite a few including:

CAT FANCIERS' ASSOCIATION, INC. (the largest)
    1805 Atlantic Avenue
    P.O. Box 1005
    Manasquan, NJ 08736-0805
    (908) 528-9797

AMERICAN CAT FANCIERS' ASSOCIATION
    P.O. Box 203
    Point Lookout, MO 65726
    (417) 334-5430

AMERICAN CAT ASSOCIATION
    8101 Katherine Avenue
    Panorama City, CA 91402
    (818) 782-6080

CAT FANCIERS' FEDERATION
    9509 Montgomery Road
    Cincinnati, OH 45242
    (513) 984-1841

In Canada:

CANADIAN CAT ASSOCIATION
      83 Kennedy Road South
      Unit 1805
      Brampton, Ontario
      L6W 3P3
      CANADA
      (416) 459-1481

The Cat Breeds

The names of the recognized purebred cat breeds tend to be misleading. The dog breed names can be, too. The Great Dane, for example, is not a Danish breed but comes from Germany. The cat breeds, though, really do play fast and loose with geography. The cats themselves are real enough but the names by which most of them are known are pure show business.

SHORTHAIR CATS

SIAMESE   possible origin, Burma or Egypt.

COLORPOINT SHORTHAIR   cross between Siamese and
Abyssinian and tabby shorthairs.

ABYSSINIAN   origin in Asia and ancient Egypt.

BURMESE   India, probably, and Burma.

RUSSIAN BLUE   quite possibly did originate in Russia.

HAVANA BROWN   developed in the United Kingdom and
the United States.

FOREIGN AND ORIENTAL SHORTHAIR   developed in the
United Kingdom and the United States.

EGYPTIAN MAU   probably Egyptian in origin.

ORIENTAL SPOTTED TABBY   United Kingdom development from the Egyptian Mau.

KORAT   from Thailand, almost certainly.

BOMBAY   in the United States, Burmese cross with black
American Shorthairs.

REX   Cornwall, England—developed from a single sport
born there.

BRITISH SHORTHAIR   from the United Kingdom.

AMERICAN SHORTHAIR   developed in America from British stock.

AMERICAN WIREHAIR   the United Kingdom and the
United States.

SCOTTISH FOLD   a mutation that occurred in Scotland.

MANX   originated in Spain or the Middle East, it is believed.

JAPANESE BOBTAIL   from Japan, as far as is known.

EXOTIC SHORTHAIR   developed in the United States for
the most part.

SOMALI developed from British Abyssinians, it is thought, in Great Britain.

LONGHAIR CATS

PERSIAN/LONGHAIR possibly first came from Turkey and/ or Armenia—once known as Angora—developed in France and the United Kingdom.

HIMALAYAN/COLORPOINT LONGHAIR developed in England after false starts in Sweden and the United States.

BIRMAN probably originated in Burma and then developed in France.

BALINESE developed in the United States from the Siamese.

TURKISH ANGORA from Turkey originally.

MAINE COON origin unknown—brought to Maine by seamen.

There are many subsets of breeds like the Siamese and the Persian/Longhair and the various shorthair breeds. The breeds listed here, however, for show purposes, are the established breeds recognized by the Cat Fanciers Association, Inc.

And then, of course, there are the cats of Thistle Hill Farm.

Protecting Your Cat Against Disease

Fortunately, the diseases most likely to sicken or kill your cat can be prevented by immunization. The vaccines available are generally very good and certainly worth the investment. It takes just a little bit of money and no more time than a visit to your veterinarian to greatly enhance and probably lengthen your pet's life.

We all love charts that tell us which shot, when, and how often, but it is better if you go along with the advice of your pet's own doctor. Some of the diseases have several different vaccines available and when and how often shots should be given depends on the vaccine used by your veterinarian, as well as the age and general health of your cat. These, though, are the diseases against which you can literally buy protection:

FELINE PANLEUKOPENIA. Also known as feline distemper (confusing: not related to canine distemper) this viral disease is a potential killer. Two kinds of protection are available: live and killed vaccines. Boosters are recommended on a schedule established by your veterinarian. This virus is the most serious cause of feline enteritis.

RESPIRATORY DISEASE. Upper respiratory infections are highly contagious in cats and three different kinds of protection are available. Your veterinarian will have a preference.

FELINE LEUKEMIA. Once a major killer. Highly infectious. Despite the freak occurrence at Thistle Hill Farm the vaccine is generally reliable. No cat should be without it.

RABIES. This disease is 100 percent fatal, and protection is essential. Contrary to what many people believe, cats are just as susceptible as dogs. The protection offered by the vaccine is very good, and once it has been given your cat is safe for at least a year even if exposed. Ask your vet. In some parts of the United States and Canada it is critical that your cat be protected both early and always.

How to Immortalize
Your Pets

Our pets give us so much, but they cannot be immortal for us, not even very long-lived. There is a small way that you can keep your part active in history even after you yourself are gone. Send a photograph of your pet with any information you want listed with a check for $15.00 made out to the ASPCA to:

> Cindy Adams
> Pet Memory Book
> ASPCA
> 424 East 92nd Street
> New York, New York 10128

Someday, a hundred years from now, someone will come across a picture of your special friend, look admiringly at him or her, and your pet, for that moment, will live again.

About the Author

ROGER CARAS is the eighteenth president of the American Society for the Prevention of Cruelty to Animals, the ASPCA, the oldest humane organization in the Western Hemisphere. Prior to taking on the leadership of the "A" he was with ABC Network News for seventeen years, the only television correspondent to have the title "Special Correspondent for Animals and the Environment." He is the author of over sixty books.